Montrose
Arbroath
Carnoustie
Broughty Ferry
St. Andrews
Fife Ness
Crail
Anstruther
St Monans
Elie
Dundee
Forfar
Glamis
Kirriemuir
N. Berwick
Kirkcaldy
Burntisland
Dunbar
St. Abbs
Eyemouth
Berwick
Musselburgh
Dunfermline
S. Queensferry
EDINBURGH

THE BREEZY COAST

THE BREEZY COAST

(Berwick to John o' Groats)

by

A. A. THOMSON

HERBERT JENKINS LIMITED
3 YORK STREET ST. JAMES'S
LONDON S.W.1

First Printing, 1932

Printed in Great Britain by Butler & Tanner Ltd., Frome and London

Photo by Valentine & Sons, Ltd.

DUNFERMLINE ABBEY, FROM PITTENCRIEFF GLEN

'' Here sleeps Scotland's greatest hero . . .''

CONTENTS

ILLUSTRATIONS

THE BREEZY COAST

I

THE CASTLE OF BLACK AGNES

"Leaving the fine old English town of Berwick behind us," said Balaam, "we start for the unknown."

No doubt it is a monstrous thing that my cynical friend should be able to refer to Berwick-on-Tweed as an English town, but if we were to remain and fight that particularly dour Border battle, there was no saying when the campaign would end. Very reluctantly I consented to give Berwick to Balaam, and proceeded towards the Border, which, as I pointed out, was three or four miles farther north than it had any right to be.

The slope of Halidon Hill stretched away on our left—that hill up which a Scottish army once struggled under a death-hail of arrows from Edward III's bowmen—

> . . . the fatal hail-shower,
> The storm of England's wrath, sure, swift, resistless,
> Which no mail-coat can brook.

Bravely as they came on, the clothyard shafts mowed them down, and the wearied handful that reached the crest were trampled beneath the horses of the English cavalry. This sad day marked one of the swift changes in the life of that shuttlecock town, Berwick, for the English, flushed with victory, marched down the hill and took it. So many mediæval battles seem to have been fought on hills and, for the life of me, I have never been able to understand why the attacking army should ever imagine that it could dislodge the enemy. The fellow who was on the hill first had such a natural advantage in position that he invariably won the battle. The other fellow, so to speak, merely threw his wicket away. If I had found my enemy holding an impregnable position of that kind, I would, like Dogberry, have let him stay there, and thanked God that I was rid of such a knave.

There is little to tell you that you have crossed the Border. You slip over it almost imperceptibly, but soon afterwards—at Burnmouth—you have your first choice between the main, straight road to Edinburgh and the jollier road that hugs the coast. As we had set out with the deliberate intention of being coast-huggers, we swung off to the right at Burnmouth along a road that makes a fine marine drive, running high above a steep slope down to the sea. There are spring days when the grim, grey North Sea loses all its terrors. On such a day as we drove into Scotland, it was a lovely blue, not, perhaps, the enamelled blue of the Mediterranean, but a soft and fresh and friendly colour, in harmony with the green of the steep shore and the brighter blue of the sky.

As we were making for the little town of Eyemouth, a sturdy countryman hailed us. He had missed the Eyemouth bus and would we be so good as to give him a lift? We signified that we would be so good, and, ensconced in our back seat, the little man discoursed with great volubility. Were we holiday-making? Then why go farther than Eyemouth? A grand wee place, though he said it who had lived there all his life. For pleesure, we were to understand. Not for business, of course. As friends of his—and now that we had given him a lift, we were his friends for life—he would not advise us to hope that we would get much business out of the place. The fishing was in a bad way— an awfu' bad way. There was no telling what the herring and the mackerel were coming to. Would we believe him, herring were down to hauf-a-croon a basket.

We expressed sincere sympathy and, on my own account, I gave him a patriotic promise to eat more fish, if that would do his native town any good.

"I see," he said, keeking over my shoulder in the friendliest manner imaginable, "that you're putting me down in shorthand. A grand accomplishment, that."

Modestly, I denied the charge. I am no short-hand expert. I was transcribing a few notes on the scenery in my own execrable longhand—a hand to which Balaam's fierce driving may have added a hieroglyphic or Pitmanesque touch. But our friend swept my denials aside as false modesty.

"Ay," he repeated admiringly, "a grand accomplishment. I'll bet I left the school a long time before you did. It's one of the chief regrets of my life," he added wistfully, "that I never got as far as the shorthand."

He was still effusive in his thanks when we set him down just outside the town.

"Don't forget to ask for me if you're this way again," he beamed. "I'm well known here. I'm the organist at the chapel and I can put ye in the way of all the pleesure that's goin'. Ye'll have a fine time, if ye're holidaying. But, business? No. Not with the herrin's at hauf-a-croon a basket. Good-bye and good luck to ye."

Eyemouth is a pleasant little huddle of grey stone houses and red-tiled roofs. If the word were not forbidden, I might have called it quaint. Certain glimpses of it reminded one of Brixham, most delightful of Devon fishing towns. Balaam said it was more like *his* idea of a Breton fishing village than most of the fishing villages he had seen in Brittany last year.

"I love the way in which the sun strikes those red roofs," I said. "It's a gorgeous bit of colour."

"Gorgeous," agreed Balaam. (When Balaam agrees with you without argument, it is a sign that the conversation has reached a danger-point.) "The sun on those red roofs makes as fine a bit of colour as we're likely to see in Scotland, but let me tell you that the red roofs are not on your beautiful old cottages. It's the tiles of the new council-houses that give the fine colour."

14

This was true enough, and a great triumph for Balaam, who pretends to find no good in anything that is old. Indeed, as we passed through the town and looked back on it from the rising road beyond, the effect was even more striking. No colour could have been finer than that of the sunlight on those despised roofs.

The road, keeping parallel to the sea but some distance away from it, runs towards Coldingham, where remain the ruined chancel and the grey skeleton of an ancient priory. The first nunnery was built by sweet St. Ebba in far-off Saxon times, but fierce Norse pirates, raiding the coast with sword and torch, razed it to the ground. In early Norman days a Benedictine priory was built upon the same spot and there the cloistered life was peacefully lived until the ruffian Hertford, who must have seemed like Anti-Christ to the simple souls of the time, came down upon Coldingham like a wolf on the fold, and burned it as he burned fair Melrose and the other border abbeys. Cromwell in his northern marches did the priory some despite also, but he never had in his heart that dull brutishness and motiveless malevolence which seem to have been the mainspring of Hertford's evil character.

Scott's highly-coloured romance, *Marmion*, owes to Coldingham one of its most powerful episodes, which recounts the dread fate meted out by ecclesiastical justice, to Constance of Beverley, the frail and beautiful nun who had broken her vows and

15

bartered her hopes of heaven for earthly love's sake. The passages describing her trial and punishment are stark and grim. Because she had forfeited "all here, and all beyond the grave," she was sentenced, along with the renegade monk who had betrayed her secret, to a living death, walled up in a secret dungeon.

> Yet well the luckless wretch might shriek,
> Well might her paleness terror speak!
> For there were seen in that dark wall,
> Two niches, narrow, deep and tall.
> Who enters at such grisly door
> Shall ne'er, I ween, find exit more.

The poet, for his own purposes, places the story in the castle-dungeons on Holy Island, but such a tragedy was actually enacted at Coldingham, for in Scott's time the skeleton of a woman was found there in such a position as told that she had been sealed up, alive, in the wall.

"And that," said Balaam, "by the gentle, holy monks you feel so sorry for."

I can only hope not.

From Coldingham we struck out sharply towards the sea again by lanes as steep and winding as ever wandered through Devon. There we found a little village perched like an eagle's nest upon the cliff-side. Down below us lay a pretty little rock-set harbour, for all the world like a tiny corner of Brittany, and, away on our left, towered the tremendous promontory of St. Abb's Head, a monster of jagged

Photo by Valentine & Sons, Ltd.

ST. ABB'S HEAD

"The tremendous promontory, a monster of jagged rock . . ."

rock. In and out of the rocky ledges sea-birds were ceaselessly flying, wheeling and swooping; sometimes hovering like a white cloud against black rock or blue sky. The deafening clamour of their screams cut the peaceful air like a knife-blade. It was no gentle moaning but the wild, tortured cry of thousands of lost souls. The village itself is so charming that it might compensate for the eerie noises of the gulls, and, of course, the gulls may not always be so vocal as when we were there, but I must admit that they went near to spoiling (for me) an otherwise perfect spot.

Balaam, from sheer contrariety, took a more tolerant view.

"You're over-sensitive," he said. "I admit those birds sound like souls in hell, but a generation that has been trained to endure wireless sopranos oughtn't to flinch from a little thing like that."

Farther along the coast stands the broken shell of the ruggedly named Fast Castle, which Scott, in *The Bride of Lammermuir*, re-named Wolf's Crag. There lived the decaying family of Ravenswood, where the last sad squire of his race was attended by that prince of faithful, cantankerous servant-tyrants, Caleb Balderstone. In the eerie atmosphere of the storm-swept cliffs and the decaying, half-ruined house, the scene is set, and here, too, Scott has the chance to give one of his inimitable character studies. Scott, perhaps mistakenly, thought himself very good at what he called the "big bow-wow strain", but, while nowadays the bow-wow strain may seem painfully dull, his genius for the delineation of real character with all its quirks and cranks and oddities, remains as fresh as ever. And Caleb Balderstone is as real as a Dickens character, that is to say, much more real than most of the people we meet every day. Scott describes Wolf's Crag as being like the nest of some sea-eagle, a solitary and naked tower on a beetling cliff. Even then it was partly in ruins, and the novelist's words might still stand in winter time: "The sombrous and heavy sound of the billows, successively dashing against the rocky beach at a profound distance beneath, was to the ear what the landscape was to the eye—a symbol of unvaried and monotonous melancholy, not unmingled with horror."

The waves, however, were not "sombrous" on a spring morning and we refused to give ourselves up to melancholy.

We were now passing along a stretch of country that might have been a bit of the real Highlands. For the moment not a single tree was in sight. Brown heather moorland rolled away towards the sea and rough heather bents were on our left, too. Dotted along the moorland were stacks of peat, looking as though they had been cut long ago and left standing. It was a scene we scarcely expected to see until we reached the far North, but it was not to last very long. Soon, as we ran along the high road, the moorland merged down the slope, towards a chessboard of beautifully tilled little fields. The moment of moorland was gone, and the whole scene opened out into an expanse of glowing colour. Here was symphony of brilliant blue, red and green —colours as oddly set in dabs and splashes as a cushion in a Chelsea studio. Each colour stood up sharply, the blue of sky and sea, the green of rolling meadows and the bricky Devonian red of the ploughed land. The road still ran on like a sweeping marine drive, sometimes almost on the cliff's edge and sometimes above a sweeping slope of red and green. Here this brightly coloured slope would be intersected by little winding lanes and there by deep chines, running down to the shore.

Near Cockburnspath our byway met the main Dunbar road again and here we were in the Lammermuir country. Here lay, in the old days, the main military and droving road from Scotland into England. If you could hold the road about this point, you were pretty sure of preventing your enemy from moving. When Cromwell, before the Battle of Dunbar, found this position strongly held by the Scots, he said: "We cannot pass, save almost by a miracle." But then Cromwell was the sort of general to whom miracles had a habit of happening.

The Battle of Dunbar, one of Cromwell's crowning mercies, was fought not at Dunbar, but on the low ground by Broxburn Glen. The grizzled veteran, Leslie, Cromwell's one-time ally, whose home we were to see in Fife, had espoused the cause of Charles II and with an army of old campaigners held a position on Doon Hill from which no military power could have moved him. Cromwell's small army, ill-provisioned and wasted by casualties and disease, lay at a grievous disadvantage, the road in front of them impregnably barred, and their backs to the sea. Only a miracle could save the English from swift destruction if they attacked, or slow starvation if they remained where they were.

A miracle was required. A miracle happened. It was one of the disadvantages of a Covenanting army that it always carried with it a cohort of ministers—men of fanatical courage but not necessarily skilled in the strategy of worldly warfare. They believed implicitly that they had the ear of the God of Battles, Who, they contended, had given them direct orders to rush down the hill and cut the enemy to pieces. Leslie, swayed by the less intoxicating considerations of sober sense, shook his grizzled head, but the warriors of the Covenant, denouncing him as a faintheart and a Laodicean, prevailed upon him to go against his own shrewder judgment. Down the hill he marched to his destruction.

"The Lord," cried Cromwell in triumph, "hath delivered them into our hands!" His horsemen, men of iron discipline and inspired religious zeal, charged in an overwhelming wave upon Leslie's unprotected wing, mowing it down like corn and hurling its broken fragments into the huddled main body, hemmed in between river and high ground. A disciplined army broke, swayed and became a rabble. It was not defeat; it was overwhelming disaster. Three thousand brave Scots lay dead on the stricken field and three times as many were taken prisoner. So it was made certain that King Charles, for another ten years at least, should set off "on his travels again."

The Edinburgh road takes the third side of a triangle, the other two sides of which form the way in and out of Dunbar. To Dunbar we went for several reasons, but mainly to see the place where a delightful Amazon, named Black Agnes, once fought off the English with gay and laughing gallantry. Dunbar has managed, in a way that few towns achieve, to make the best of both worlds— the old and the new. That is, it has turned itself into a thriving summer resort with excellent golf for those who want it, and yet it has not lost its character as an ancient seaport, with a history of battles and sieges, loves and hates, escapes and adventures, that stretches dimly back into Saxon times. There is a long, ancient, cobbled street that reminds you of some old Norman town, and the side streets are clean and wide. The church is a great red building, imposing to the eye, but I am told that it is not really very old. Most of it that you see was rebuilt only a hundred years ago. The harbour, like almost everything else we saw that day, glowed with colour—especially with that rich red, which you have heard of so much in songs about Red Devon by the Sea. Red harbour. White lighthouse. Blue sky. Dunbar is determined to be patriotic or nothing.

The battered skeleton of Dunbar Castle frowns down from a lofty rock upon the pretty red harbour. You can imagine that it was just as nearly impregnable as any castle might be in a country where Robert the Bruce was once king. It belonged, the most ancient records tell us, to an eleventh-century forebear of the Earls of March. It gave shelter— and this was a rather weakly sentimental act on the part of a castle not much given to sentiment—to the recreant Edward of England, fleeing from defeat and disgrace at Bannockburn. He escaped from Dunbar in a fishing-boat and I hope he had a most unpleasant voyage.

Mary, sad Queen of Scots, knew Dunbar Castle well. It was there that she fled, after the murder at Holyrood of her musician secretary, Rizzio, along with her husband Darnley, who had consented to that brutal deed. When her honeymoon at Borthwick Castle with the evil Bothwell was interrupted, he fled to Dunbar, and she followed him, romantic and foolishly faithful, disguised as a page.

But, stirring as were its other adventures, the most thrilling episode in the castle's history came a quarter of a century after Edward's escape, when the Countess of March heroically held it against the English. The triumph of Scotland in the wars of liberty rested heavily on the shoulders of one man. When Bruce died, there was no giant to carry on his work. Scotland lacked his godlike spirit and his iron hand. Randolph, Earl of Moray, who was chosen regent during the minority of Bruce's son, David, was a gallant soldier and a just man, but he was no demi-god. His successor was neither gallant nor just, and so the splendid national fabric that Bruce had built began to crack. The Baliol faction began to raise its head, and civil war, abetted, needless to say, by the English, tore the country in two. Dupplin Moor was fought and lost, and a hated Baliol was crowned at Scone.

After Halidon Hill, an even bloodier defeat, the spirit of the Scots for a time was broken, and only here and there did an odd castle hold gallantly out against Edward's ravaging armies. Of these Dunbar was the bravest. Not for nothing was Black Agnes, Countess of March, the daughter of Bruce's brave Randolph. While her husband was fighting for his hunted King, she held the castle with a handful of men, against attacks from sea and land.

Her dark proud eyes looked down disdainfully from the battlements upon the invaders, and her weapons—reinforcing the arrows of her bowmen—were woman's weapons of flashing raillery and flaming scorn. The great clumsy catapults of the besieging forces hurled massive rocks against the castle walls, but Black Agnes greeted the missiles with contemptuous laughter. She treated the fierce attacks of the English as though they were nothing but childish games. With her gentlewomen, attired in holiday array, she walked the battlements, and when some jagged rock crashed against the wall, she would bid her maids wipe the spot clean with a linen cloth. "For," said she, "I must keep my castle unsullied by these English, who, after all, can raise little more dust than a napkin can wipe away."

Salisbury, the English commander, then brought up a curious engine which, in those days, must have been regarded as a masterpiece of the heavy artillery-man's art. It was a mantlet-tower, rolled up on clumsy wheels to the castle wall, and while the attacking army strove to undermine the foundations, its broad, curved back gave them a certain amount of protection from the stones, arrows and boiling oil hurled down by the welcoming defenders within. It attempted, you see, a kind of crude combination between the labours of the Tank Corps and the Sappers and Miners. When Black Agnes saw this ugly engine approaching, she gazed upon its broad "sowbackit" roof with derision and called out shrilly to Salisbury:

> "Beware, Montagow,
> For farrow shall thy sow!"

An ungentlewomanly remark, perhaps, but a true prophecy. As the sow's back came up under the battlements, Black Agnes gave the signal and a great mountain of rock, as if it had been a bomb from

an aeroplane, was dropped neatly on to the roof
and went crashing through it. Out from beneath
the wreckage, the English soldiers came scurrying
for their lives in all directions, while Agnes and her
maids called out in delighted chorus: "The English
sow has farrowed!"

No besieger was ever safe, for the archers of Black
Agnes were deadly in their aim. More than one
English knight fell, pierced through three-fold mail.
"There," said Salisbury grimly, "goes one of my
lady's love-tokens. Her love-shafts are so ardent
that they pierce through to the heart."

The castle held out for nineteen weeks, and when
the garrison was at its last gasp, the brave Alexander
of Dalwolsy slipped through the blockade of the
English ships around the harbour, bringing in
reinforcements and (what was needed more) a goodly
supply of rations. Whereupon the English commander, bitterly hurt by the indignity of the whole
affair, raised the siege and went sulkily off home.

> She kept a stir in tower and trench,
> That brawling boisterous Scottish wench;
> Came I early, came I late,
> I found Black Agnes at the gate.

As he rode disconsolately away, you may be quite
certain that Agnes had the last word, following him
with maddening laughter.

He was only a man, and what are men after all?
So when I read in my morning paper of the exploits

of that brawling, boisterous person who is called
The Modern Girl, I think of gay and gallant Black
Agnes and refuse to become excited.

We came out on the north side of Dunbar by
way of Belhaven and Westbarns, and were now
fairly launched upon a route which is golf-links,
golf-links all the way.

"Golf," said Balaam. "We now approach the
confines of an empire on which the sun never—or
hardly ever—sets. It is a solemn thought."

II

LINKLAND

Golf, golf, golf,—is all the story!
  In despair my over-burdened spirit sinks,
Till I wish that every golfer was in glory,
  And I pray the sea may overflow the links.

                          R. F. MURRAY.

FAR away to our right stretched a coast-line of
gently undulating green and brown—what
Balaam called a "duney" coast. What other people
call dunes, Eastern Scotland calls links, a word
which the English mind associates only with golf.
The ignorant might toy with the notions of "links"
and "golf," wondering, as primitive biologists
wondered of the hen and the egg, which came
first. There is no need for wonder. The links undoubtedly came first, and golf (for good or evil)
came comparatively late in the history of mankind.
If the cynical poet genuinely wishes that every
golfer was in glory, he could not wish him in any
better place than this coast, for here the golfer
is undoubtedly *in his glory*.

Whatever its associations, a coast consisting of
green and golden links is a jolly thing in itself, and
while Balaam might be impressed by its semi-sacred
suggestions of driver and putter, I was quite contented to love it for itself alone. Perhaps we were
specially blessed in our day. All along this fringe

of "linkland," we had no hint of mist or greyness, no sharp reminder that the wind can blow snell from the sea. The country was everywhere clean and bright, sharply outlined under a sky of which sunny Italy need not have been ashamed.

The first and most outstanding landmark on this coast-road is the ruined castle of Tantallon. I say "ruined," because the war-engines of centuries and the more insidious artillery of Time itself have wrought all the evil in their power against this tremendous red keep, but it is no pathetic fragment, crumbling in decay. Much of it remains, standing as defiantly as ever on its high rock-bound eyrie, and will remain, when you and I are dead and gone. Of all the castles that perch upon impregnable sea-cliffs, I do not know one which breathes quite the same spirit of arrogant defiance towards elements or human enemies. There it stands, doubly moated on the landward side and glowering across the blue water at the craggy outline of the Bass Rock. The clearness of the sunny air on the day we drove along suggested that the Bass Rock was only a stone's throw away. But the distance is no stone's throw. When, in the old days, the local folk wished to suggest the period of the Greek Kalends, they placed it at a time when some supernatural power should "Build a brig to the Bass and ding doon Tantallon." Neither of these unlikely happenings have occurred yet, though Monk, round about the time of the Battle of Dunbar, made a stout attempt to ding the

TANTALLON CASTLE AND THE BASS ROCK

"Build a brig to the Bass, ding doon Tantallon . . ."

Photo by Valentine & Sons, Ltd.

castle doon. Even the reasonably heavy artillery of that day made less impression on those gaunt red walls than it would upon other castles, and you may imagine that in earlier days, before siege-guns became a serious armament, Tantallon was the despair of beleaguering commanders. Tantallon could have laughed at Salisbury's "English sow" and Heath-Robinson ordnance of that kind, even more shrilly than did Black Agnes. For centuries Tantallon was the stronghold of that swart and turbulent family, the Douglases, who cared little for God or man and could often be as cruel as they were always brave. To the castle itself the Douglases would seem to have imparted some of the fearless courage and fierce arrogance of their race. Deeply embedded in those tremendous walls were honeycombed passages and dark eerie dungeons where the light of day never penetrated, and when a Douglas flung his prisoner into these cheerless, airless catacombs, that luckless captive could but resign himself to a living death. What a massive bulk the castle has, three sides to the sea and one to the land! It is scarcely less impressive to-day, than when Scott described it in *Marmion*:

> . . . . Bulwark and bartizan and line
> And bastion, tower, and vantage coign;
> Above the booming ocean leant
> The far-projecting battlement;
> The billows burst in ceaseless flow
> Upon the precipice below.

> Where'er Tantallon faced the land,
> Gateworks and walls were strongly manned;
> No need upon the sea-girt side;
> The steepy rock, the frantic tide,
> Approach of human step denied. . . .

The ocean was not booming to any great extent, but you could easily imagine that it might, and you had only to look over "the steepy rock" to realise how little need there was for sentinels upon "the sea-girt side."

In a thrilling passage of the poem, Scott endues his hero-villain, Marmion, with the incredible courage to "beard the lion in his den, the Douglas in his hall."

But Marmion, it scarcely need be said, was a fictitious character, and no genuine record exists, so far as I am aware, of any stranger having bearded the Douglas in his hall and escaped with his life. All the probabilities are that he would have paid for his temerity by leaving his bones a-bleaching in the darker corners of the lions'-den. . . .

> Lord Marmion turned,—well was his need,
> And dashed the rowels in his steed,
> Like arrow through the archway sprung,
> The ponderous gate behind him rung:
> To pass there was such scanty room,
> The bar, descending, razed his plume.
> The steed along the drawbridge flies,
> Just as it trembled on the rise . . .
> And when Lord Marmion reached his band,
> He halts and turns with clenched hand,
> And shout of loud defiance pours
> And shook his gauntlet at the towers . . .

But Balaam shook his head when I recited to him this thundering passage that has stuck in my head since schooldays.

"No," he said, "I'd like to think that an Englishman got away with it, but I'm very doubtful."

The Bass Rock is to this coast what Ailsa Craig is to the Ayrshire seaboard—a steep, gaunt mass rising craggily out of the water, visible at great distances and dominating the seascape wherever it is in view. You may travel what you imagine to be a very long way, but as long as you have an uninterrupted view of the coast-line, there you will see the Bass Rock glaring at you, apparently as near as ever. It reminds you of races that children sometimes have with the moon, scurrying along the country road and still finding that it keeps up with them, however fast they run. Like Ailsa, it is the haunt of clouds of seabirds—especially the solan geese, of which you will read in *Catriona*.

The slopes of the rock rise so steeply that it looks at first sight from the shore as though no boat could ever land there, but men still go there to shoot the solan geese, and the fortress there was in Covenanting times the grimmest of all prisons. The very name of the Bass was a thing to strike cold fear into the heart of even the stoutest Whig, and imprisonment on the Bass, with its cruelty and unearthly loneliness amid the eerie crying of the sea-birds, held something of the terror that was worse than death. The Prophet Peden, whose face was like

31

the day of judgment and whom his enemies feared and hated because they thought that he had the power to will an evil fate upon them, was imprisoned for years upon the rock, but succeeded by sheer bravery of spirit in surviving its hardships.

Ten years later, when William of Orange landed and King James fled in ignominy, the tables were turned, and certain followers of the old régime were imprisoned on the Rock. Less than a score or so of gay young cavaliers overpowered their gaolers, and for three years held out in a sort of frolic defiance against a government which had its hands far too full of weightier matters to attend to them. At the end of that time King William's troops stormed and destroyed the fort and the picnic rebellion was summarily ended. But it must have been great fun while it lasted.

The most thrilling story of the Bass, of course, is the account of David Balfour's incarceration there, for devious political reasons, in the matchless romance of *Catriona*. There we read the tale of Tod Lapraik told by David's grim gaoler, Black Andie, one of the most terrifying tales ever set down in literature. It is the tale of the soul of a weaver that would leave his body and, in the form of a warlock, dance upon the Bass to the skirling of the solan geese. Sandie Fletcher shot at the warlock, having placed a silver tester in his gun, along with the leaden bullets. As the shot rang out, the warlock disappeared, but when they came home, they found Tod Lapraik, the weaver, dead at his loom, with a silver tester in his heart.

"Ay," as Andie would say, "*it's an unco place, the Bass*."

We looked out from beside the wall of Tantallon and gazed across, beyond the Bass and May Island, towards the coast of Fife. At first glimpse it did not appear, as in Carlyle's memorable description, a mass of "projecting rock promontories with which that coast is necked and vandyked as far as the eye can reach," but a pearly ghost of a line, distantly enchanting, infinitely mysterious, a coast that might have been the magic sea-coast of Bohemia.

Along a sweeping curve of coast we continued, finding landscape and seascape dominated by the great green mound of Berwick Law, a perfect pocket-mountain. There, if anywhere, was the place for a mediæval stronghold that would have been more impregnable than even Tantallon. Its top would have been a position that three men and a boy could have held against an army, unless, of course, the besiegers had seventeen-inch guns that could blow the whole Berwick Law itself into the sea. The summit has no castle but the ruins of a look-out tower, whence watchers eagerly scanned the sea for the approach of Boney's flat-bottomed boats which were to land on the east coast and consummate the Napoleonic invasion of Britain. This was the time when all patriotic citizens joined the Volunteers for the honour of guarding their native shores and when Walter Scott, in spite of his lame foot, was a keen and active officer in the Yeomanry. The young man from whom we purchased petrol under the shadow of Berwick Law told us that on the summit were also set up, in a grim arch, the jawbones of a whale, but he omitted to inform us how the whale found its way there.

North Berwick is the inner shrine of this golfing coast. Apart from the exalted and select hierarchy who probably haunt St. Andrews, it is safe to say that good golfers go to North Berwick when they die. Quite a number of them go before, but these visits are foretastes, as it were, of the life of perfect bliss which is to come. Here golf is no game, but a sacred ritual. The town is as much under the influence of a solemn idea as Mecca or Medina. The favourite inscription over a local shop is not the familiar sign of the butcher, baker, or candle-stick-maker, but the awe-inspiring legend:

J. McSo-and-so, CLUBMAKER.

It is very difficult for the most irreverent mind not to be impressed. For myself, I am prepared to bow from courtesy to the custom of the country, and Balaam, though the most irreverent soul I know, is a golfer himself, so both of us were suitably impressed by North Berwick. As I stood on the edge of West Links, I could not help reflecting on the remark made by the heroine of one of P. G. Wodehouse's stories—"But after all, golf is only a game, isn't it!"—and of the horror such a remark naturally evoked. If you said a thing like that at North Berwick, burning brassies would fall from Heaven and utterly destroy you.

The town itself, neat and sedate but not in the least unfriendly, grows on you. The quietness of its streets and the trimness of its fine sweeping greensward make you feel slightly ashamed that you may ever have thought of the noisier pleasures of such places as Southend-on-Sea. The old fishing harbour divides the two charming bays rather like the bridge of a pair of spectacles, and in each direction you will find a fine beach, a golf course, and as fine a supply of invigorating sea air as you will find anywhere on the coast. This east coast air has a tang of its own, fresh and salty, that heartens and invigorates. On such a day as we passed along West Bay, it is the very breath of Spring.

The next village we passed was remarkable because it drew from Balaam an unwonted enthusiasm. Of my own enthusiasm in general, I am slightly ashamed. I am, as I have said before, all too prone to like things and people, when a more critical attitude would be fitting. This attitude, I am prepared to admit, is a vice rather than a virtue, because criticising and disliking and quarrelling are things which demand from me a stern moral effort which I am much too indolent or timid to put forth. Conceding all this, I am not ashamed to be enthusiastic about Dirleton, which, if I never praise a place again, is as lovely a village as any in Scotland. How, with some pretence to a knowledge of Scotland's lovely places, I have not come on it before, is difficult to explain. Other places that are not one half so attractive as Dirleton have been extravagantly praised and with infinitely less reason. You come upon it quite unexpectedly. There it is, the sleepy village, with its green, its castle, its old church and cluster of cottages, as perfectly composed a picture as though it had sprung fresh from the imagination of a great artist. Up and down the country there are many pretty villages—I live in a pretty village myself—but nowhere have I seen a place where, as at Dirleton, all the notions of all the dream-villages that ever existed were so simply and perfectly blended. It was as though some cosmic dramatist had written Scene One: The Village Green. Enter a Maiden singing. . . .

"How very lovely," I said, as we stopped to look. Balaam was genuinely impressed.

"How very English," he said. "I mean it. I don't admit—and neither would you if you were honest—that the average Scotch village is attractive in the least. Not, at any rate, in the sense that almost every English village, with its thatched roofs and odd queer corners and its general air of sleepy cosiness, can be attractive. The average Scotch village is like the average Scotchman—cold, angular and unfriendly. It has one straight, stony street—clean and tidy, I grant you—and the whole thing, quite apart from the slate roofs, which are an abomination, is featureless and dull. But here—" Balaam was in grave danger of waxing lyrical— "you have everything good and nothing Scotch, a wide green, sleeping in the sunshine, a really good church and cottages which look like cottages and not just whitewashed buts-and-bens. It has the genuine English country atmosphere."

I left the heretic to his heresies, for while his theories were shocking, his facts were indisputable. If a countryside of perfect villages had to be formed, Dirleton would undoubtedly be there as Exhibit A.

After Dirleton we came, past smiling, well-tilled fields, out near the sea again. Linkland was again in evidence, as though the coast-line were one long series of sandy, but not too difficult, hazards. We passed the neat, trim suburb of Gullane—with links on our right nearly all the way—and Aberlady, where, in a little harbour, we saw the bleaching ribs of an old fishing-boat. There were links on each side of the road now, with bright golden sands beyond, on our right. What a place for picnics! There, on holiday afternoons, an infinite number of parties can park and camp and enjoy sea, air and sun, without getting in each other's way. The temptation to dislike your fellow-creatures comes mainly from having to be cooped up with them in a cramped space. Here was an essentially friendly and human place, for there was room for all to enjoy themselves.

After the long "linky" coastal stretch, which might be described as the picnickers' paradise, we struck a rather bad industrial patch, where streets were narrow and the wheels of pit-heads appeared on the edge of the sea. I do not know whether these coal-mines go right out under the sea. I should think it extremely likely that they do. A little way inland from these unromantic parts was fought one of the most romantic battles in Scottish history. It was said of Bonnie Prince Charlie that he could live on a dry crust, sleep on pease-straw, eat a dinner in four minutes, and win a battle in five. Prestonpans was one of his five-minute battles —an engagement in which the whirling dash of his Highlanders simply swept their ponderous, slow-moving enemies off the face of the earth. The vital part of the onset lasted for little more than five minutes. King George's troops could not have been more effectually routed if the battle had lasted ten hours. It was the old story of the Highland dash which, fierce as a mountain torrent, could win almost every battle but could not, in the long run, consolidate a campaign.

Prestonpans was, perhaps, the peak of Prince Charlie's short-lived triumph. He had taken Edinburgh, almost without resistance, and there he was given the most loving welcome that exiled Prince Charming ever had. Once more a Stuart was at Holyrood. Colour and romance lived again after drab times. Music and laughter reigned again in the old palace and loyal hearts beat high. But the Prince knew well that it was no time for merry-making, for the royal troops, under Sir John Cope, had landed at Dunbar and were marching towards Haddington. Placing himself at the head of his troops, he marched them out through Duddingston and Musselburgh to meet the enemy. Drawing his sword, he waved it aloft and cried, with his unerring instinct for the inspiring phrase: "Gentlemen, I have flung away the scabbard!" When the armies came together, it was seen that Cope's forces were protected by what seemed to be an impassable swamp. Through the night the two armies lay facing one another, but in the rimy mist of the dawn, the Highlanders, guided by a Jacobite gentle-man named Anderson, who knew of a secret path-way, stole like ghosts across the morass. The curtain of mist lifted and the morning sun shone out, to reveal the Highlanders, in fierce battle array, safely posted on the hither side of the swamp. They had turned their enemy's impregnable position into one of extreme vulnerability. It was a moment of panic—panic from which Cope's men never recovered. There has never been in the world a torrent so fierce as the rush of that first Highland charge. Musket-volleys could not shake the im-petuosity of their onset. The royal troops, dazed, bewildered and panic-stricken, were mown down as they stood or tried to escape. Mown down they were, with grim literalness, for many of the wild

Highlanders wielded flashing scythes. Colonel Gardiner, bravest of the King's officers, was cut down by one of these grisly weapons. Cope himself, after vain attempts to rally the stragglers, fled from the field, and the ignominy of his flight has echoed down the years to the grimly sardonic strains of: "Hey, Johnnie Cope, are ye wauken yet?"

Yes, Prestonpans was the noontide hour in the Prince's brief day, but, even in that glory of victory, there was little real cause for exultation.

"Here, sir," said a Highland chieftain, as they rode over a field packed with the bodies of the slain, "your enemies lie at your feet."

But the Prince turned away his head.

"They are my father's subjects," he said.

Henceforth the wild impetuosity of his Highlanders was to be a liability rather than an asset.

Our road took us, past more pitheads and narrow streets, towards Musselburgh, a cobbled road and tramlines. Though we had come to a town, there were still links between the town and the sea. While an old-fashioned fishing-village can change into a town, golf goes on for ever. Flashing past, us on bicycles, we saw Loretto boys in red blazers with golf-bags slung across their backs. Old things and new mingle at Musselburgh. We passed the long narrow track of a race-course, which is also the site of the spot where Cromwell camped, after the Lord had delivered the enemy into his hand at Dunbar. So by way of the Eastern-sounding Joppa, we came to Portobello. One of my earliest recollections is wondering whereabouts in Joppa was the house of Simon the Tanner where St. Peter had his vision of the sheet let down from heaven. Another very early memory is the throaty voice of an Edinburgh porter crying: "Por-rtobello, Musselburgh *and* Dalkeith. . . . Por-rtobello, Musselburgh *and* Dalkeith." I cannot have been more than four or five when I first heard my leather-lunged friend roaring out this curious free-verse poem, but there must have been some queer cadence about it that has remained in my memory when things that I ought to remember have faded. Porto-bello saw the death of one great Scotsman. Hugh Miller, of whom I shall say more when we reach his loved Black Isle, died here, under a sad mental cloud, by his own hand. Portobello also saw the birth of one who, after Scott and Burns, has some reasonable claim to stand in the minds and the memories of the millions whenever Scotland's name is mentioned. There is a time-worn and venerable story of an Irish Papist and a Scottish Presbyterian who indulged in passionate and embittered argument—racial, political and theological. Finally the Scot flung his Parthian shot: "To hell with the Pope!" To which the Irishman retorted: "And to hell with Harry Lauder!"

If that is not a true compliment, perhaps you will tell me what is. You cannot argue about it. I have heard highbrows of the new and advanced Scottish Nationalist sort pour scorn on the appeal of Harry Lauder. I have also seen packed audiences sitting with glistening cheeks while a rich crystal-clear voice sang simply of love and home. The man holds his hearers by a golden thread; their tears and their laughter are at his lightest bidding.

"So obvious," say the highbrows.

But, you see, the call of home, the love of a lad for his lass, the love of a man for the land that bore him—all these are simple, obvious, and the poor intellectual who complains of their simple obviousness is to be pitied rather than blamed. If he cannot sing the chorus of "I love a lassie" then I am sorry for him. But I cannot help him. He is just as deficient of what is necessary to the complete good life as is a man with a wooden leg. And this is the point to remember when we are where we are: that Sir Harry Lauder was born, not at Tobermory or Killiecrankie, but at Portobello. And if the fact does not thrill you, then you are, as I feared, of the company of the spiritually woodenlegged.

And so to Edinburgh, under the shadow of the Calton Hill, with Holyrood House, dreaming wistfully of past splendours, in the valleyfold below. And then Princes Street in the lilac light of evening with Castle Rock towering above. . . . Nothing will tempt me to try the vain task of setting down

something new about Edinburgh. The world's
greatest writers have known the spell of the world's
fairest city and their books are open for all to see.
Of the old city and its high "lands"; of the grim
Castle Rock; of the Royal Mile, its whole historic
length tremulous with the ghosts of old loves and
hates, burning faiths and impassioned hopes; of
the churches where Knox thundered and the closes
where Burns wandered; of the houses in gracious
Georgian squares where the wits laughed and the
belles danced—all the good things have been said
long ago by better men. But this I will say: that
if I had a month's holiday I would not wish to
spend it better than in just walking up and down
Princes Street. Every day and at every hour of
the day, there is something fresh for to admire and
for to see. The light that falls from the sky above
the Castle Rock seems to change from hour to hour
and there is never a moment when some kind of
enchantment does not lie on the moving pageant
below.

I remember (again from that distant age when I
was four or five) when brave horses drew the trams
through the streets of Edinburgh and when, at the
bottom of steep hills, extra trace-horses, bestridden
by barefoot callants, waited to give the tram-horses
assistance in their pulling. To ride a trace-horse
seemed to me in those days the most exalted honour
that might fall to the lot of any human boy, and it
is still told against me in the family that one day I

was apprehended in the act of asking one of these urchins how much one had to pay for so glittering a privilege.

Horse-trams had their day, to be succeeded by the cable-cars which were regarded by the satirically-minded as being among the less attractive wonders of the world. Their clack and their roar reverberated noisily through gracious streets and good citizens of progressive views cursed them roundly. But Britons are nothing if not inconsistent, for I remember, when I was in Mesopotamia during the War, meeting an Edinburgh man who had been long years an exile in India. On the banks of the Tigris, near Bagdad, there was a place where you could hear the bulbul sing, but my friend had different ideas on the subject of sweet music. "Keep your bulbuls," he said. "What I want to hear is the sound of the cable-cars growling and grumbling up the Mound!"

We drove along Princes Street in the quiet of the evening and the air was very still. It is not always so. The last time I had been in Edinburgh, a biting blast had skirled down Princes Street, sweeping pedestrians off their feet, so that they staggered along in the teeth of the gale as though they were the remnants of a storming party under heavy fire. I did not see the legendary figure of the policeman, strapped to the railings by the Waverley steps, but I was granted a glimpse of something quite as impressive. I saw—surely the solemnest sight under the vault of heaven—a publisher chasing his hat.

But now there was no snell blast. The sky was an exquisite background of lilac, deepening in purple. Spires and pinnacles silhouetted themselves against it. Still deeper grew the purple till the Castle Rock stood out alone, a black outline, vast and mysterious. With every tone of changing sky came a fresh light, softer and fairer than before, till the street-lamps—which Stevenson said were as lovely as stars—gleamed out below, and sky and rocky height faded into one dim enchantment. Yes, I must have that holiday, just walking up and down Princes Street.

III

THE QUEEN'S FERRY

WE said good-bye to the Scott Monument and made a last regretful journey along Princes Street, a long cliff-wall of handsome shops on our right and a long valley of gardens on our left. Swinging away to the right at the west end of the street, we made towards the Dean Bridge, which was made by that greatest of bridge-builders, Thomas Telford. Although so near the city, the country opens out grandly, rolling away on every side, fresh and green. New suburbs are springing up on the hillsides, but, with their grey stone, they manage to fit inoffensively into the landscape, which is not always the way with bungaloid suburbs. The water of Leith, steeply wooded, runs far below the bridge, and the whole landscape of hill and glen is a continued joy to the eye.

Now we are on the famed Queensferry Road, an ancient highway which has seen history pass along like the episodes of an age-long pageant. Pict and Roman, Saxon and Norseman, warrior and serf, priest and reformer, Whig and Jacobite have all trodden its stones in leisured or hurried journeyings. Few kings of Scotland have not ridden to or from their ships by the Queensferry Road.

The queen who first gave her gracious name to the Ferry was Margaret, sister of Edgar Atheling, who, fleeing from the Norman invasion, was wrecked with her mother, brothers and sister, in a terrible storm on the shores of the Firth. The rude, uncivilised country-folk gaped in astonishment at the castaways. When Malcolm Canmore, the Scottish king, heard of the strangers upon his shores, he sent enquiries after them and, learning who they were, took horse and came to meet them in person. Almost at first sight he fell in love with the Princess Margaret. Soon he married her, and for her sweet sake, looked upon the English with a new kindliness and espoused the cause of Edgar against the Normans. Margaret's reign as Malcolm's queen ushered in what was almost the first dawn of culture among a savage race. She encouraged learning, as Alfred had done in England, and, though strive as she might, she never succeeded in teaching her rough warrior-husband to read, he liked to take her books in his hand, and would fondle those she loved best. So great was his affection for her learning that he would slyly purloin one of the favourite volumes, and return it to her, bound with gold clasps and encrusted with jewels. A charming action, surely, and scarcely to have been looked for from a fierce warrior-king.

She also fostered trade and granted privileges to merchants—especially to merchants of bright stuffs and the coloured fineries that delight the feminine eye. It is even said (though I should not care to submit so charming a notion to Balaam's raillery) that Scottish tartans first originated in this charming lady's pious passion for bright colours. Her charities were innumerable. Daily she fed nine beggar children with her own hand. She would wash the feet of beggars and wait upon the hungry poor at her own table. Thus, by her piety, she became Saint Margaret. David the First, who, for his benefactions to the Church was known as a "sair saint for the crown," often used this road, and so did the earlier Stuart kings. During all its history it has been a high-road of romance.

Blossoming trees, with all the bells and buds of May, filled the woodlands by the roadside. It was early yet in the year but soon, you could see, the woods would be a mass of living green. We had travelled previously along a coast not rich in trees, but here they were everywhere.

At Cramond Bridge the road crosses the river Almond. This bridge is an honest, modern, workmanlike affair and of no great account to the artist's eye, but, peering along the river's wooded banks, you can see away on the right an old stone brig, grey and weather-beaten. But even this is a modern affair compared with the still older brig, whereon honest Jock Howieson had his astonishing adventure with the Guid Man of Ballengiech. James the Fifth was, before sadness overtook him, a humoursome King and loved to play Haroun al-Raschid, wandering, disguised, among his poorer subjects. Walking one day by old Cramond Brig, he was set on by five robbers. Setting his back to the parapet of the bridge, he held his own gamely against unpleasant odds, but it would have gone hard with him, if the sounds of the unequal combat had not come to the ears of one Jock Howieson, a lusty labourer, who was threshing corn in the barn near by. Swinging his flail, Jock came rushing to the rescue. The ancient chronicle charges the luckless robbers with arrant cowardice, but it will be admitted that the spectacle of great rawboned Jock, whirling his murderous weapon, must have called for greater courage than usually resides in the breast of the common gangster. Incontinently they fled, leaving Jock to lead the king into the barn to rest his shaken nerves.

"And what'll ye be wanting now?" asked Jock.

"A basin of water and a towel," said the king. (A gentleman, however disguised, thinks of these things first.)

Afterwards they chatted and the king asked Jock who he was.

"Everybody knows me," replied Jock easily. "I'm Jock Howieson and I work at Braehead. It's a farm that belongs the king, who's a puir bit body, they say."

"I see. And what would you like best in the world, Jock?"

"I'd like what every honest man wants—a farm of my own. This one here is a nice bit farm," he added rather wistfully. "And who may you be, onyway?"

Then the king, as the modern phrase goes, came all over Haroun al-Raschid. "I am," he said, "the Guid Man of Ballengiech. I have a sort of job at the palace, you know. After all, you've done me a good turn. Come along on Sunday and I'll show you round. You'd like the place."

Sunday saw Jock in his best doublet and hose, enquiring for the Guid Man at the palace gate. The sentry, with a solemn wink, passed him along, and Jock grew hotter and more bothered as he stumped through gardens and courtyards, tapestried corridors and richly furnished halls. The crowds of lolling, gaily-dressed courtiers half annoyed and half intimidated him. It was with a sigh of relief that he reached the side of the soberly-dressed king.

"Fegs!" exclaimed Jock, mopping his brow. "It's grand to meet an honest man, after a' those dolled-up Frenchified bodies."

"And now," said his friend, after doing the honours of the place, "would you care to see the king?"

"I would that, but will he no' have a fit if he sees me?"

"You needn't worry about that."

"But how will I ken the wee fella when I see him?"

"That will be easy. Court etiquette demands that every man shall doff his bonnet in the royal presence, while the king keeps his on."

In the great audience-hall rank upon rank of courtiers bowed low as the two friends entered, baring their heads in reverence.

"I still don't see him," whispered Jock.

"Look round. I told you. You can tell him by his hat."

Jock glanced nervously round, started, and then burst into a loud guffaw.

"Well, love-a-duck!" he roared (or its equivalent in contemporary dialect). "There's only you and me for it!"

That was the beginning of a fine democratic friendship which gained for Jock the coveted farm of Braehead, and, for his descendants, the traditional privilege of carrying on ceremonial occasions a silver basin and an embroidered towel in the king's honour.

I like this story, partly because, whether true or legendary, it exactly interprets the pleasant British conception of kingship and manhood, and partly because it has a way of cropping up, in some form or other, wherever a king has been personally popular. The other day a friend of mine, who has lived abroad, solemnly told me the story, almost word for word, as having happened to the King of Spain.

("Just come round to the palace gate," said the king to the peasant, "and ask for Alfonso.")

Which seems to me a genuine tribute to a good story, and reminds me of the manager's remark to the young dramatist who claimed that his new play contained at least three startlingly original situations.

"They are that, laddie," said the genial manager, "*and always have been.*"

Still the spring woods were freshly green on either side of us, and soon we came by the great swooping, sloping curve of the Hawes Brae down to the Firth and down to the Ferry. A broad stretch of water lay before us, but not so broad that we could not see the line of coast-hills beyond. We had a vision of grey water and green islands, and caught a glimpse, away on the extreme left, of Ben Lomond's top towering mistily into the clouds. To our right on our own side of the firth, thickset woods came down to the shore and the slanting rays of the evening sun lit up their living green and streaked it with pure gold. Across the water, a little to the left, rose a line of cranes and derricks from the shipyards of Rosyth.

But we were gazing admiringly, not at Ben Lomond or the magic islands of the firth or the enchanted woodlands of the Rosebery policies, but upon the Forth Bridge—as surely a Wonder of the World as was the Colossus of Rhodes or the Great Pyramid. It has a genuine impressiveness which gives point to another ancient and venerable story. An old hard-bitten Scotsman stood on the quay at Queensferry.

"Ay," he said, "I've travelled the five continents and the seven seas. I've gazed on a' the works o' Man. But"—with an awed and reverent glance towards the Forth Bridge—"*I take off my bonnet to Nature, after all!*"

That is the right attitude. If you can think of

this giant skeleton as a strange phenomenon of Nature rather than as a "work o' Man," it is easier to get the thing into perspective. If you do not at first realise the size of the monster, glance upward when you hear the rattle of a train. That train— and it may well be a famous express, drawn by the most powerful type of engine known—looks exactly like the sort of train you bought for your nephew's last birthday. The sight of that train should give you a glimpse of your own relative insignificance, and put you in your place.

The ferry-boat was not due to start for another hour, but we did not find our wait in the least dull. Almost opposite the ferry stands the old Hawes Inn where the Antiquary and his companion, having driven down from Edinburgh in a decrepit coach, waited, as we were waiting, for their boat, and ate, under the auspices of a jolly host, a meal to make a hungry man's mouth water. " 'Ou, there's fish, nae doubt—that's sea-trout and caller haddocks,' said the landlord, twisting his napkin, 'and ye'll be for a mutton chop, and there's cranberry tarts, very weel preserved, and—just onything else ye like.' "

While we were waiting, a friendly A.A. man took us under his wing and pleasantly discoursed of this and that. He willingly accepted our admiration of his Forth Bridge in the spirit in which it was given, but modestly disclaimed any credit for its excellence or indeed any absolute faith in its permanence.

"Oh, ay," he said, "she'll stand a ding or two yet.

They whiles give her a bangin' when they're towing a battleship up to Rosyth—the *Tiger* gave her an awful dunt, only last week. Yes, she'll stand. But she should have come down last winter. I mind one afternoon when the storm came down so black you'd have thought it was the end of the world. You would, I'm telling ye. Ye couldn't see the Fife coast or the Rosyth cranes or the islands or anything. It was as black as the inside of a Sabbath hat. I'd have bet a shilling the bridge was going. Steel or no steel, no mortal bridge could have stood it much longer. There's six-and-a-half-million rivets in her, and every one o' them was squeaking."

"And what did you do," asked Balaam, "with the end of the world so imminently approaching?"

"I helped a drookit man to change his back wheel," said our stoic, "and then I went home to my tea."

He pointed out the islands in the firth.

"You'll have heard the wee joke," he said, "that the folk round here try on the English. It's not much of a joke, really. I say to you: 'How many inches are there from here to the sea?' And you say——"

"We'll buy it," I said politely.

"And then I say: 'Just three.' Three inches, you see, Inchgarvie, Inchcolm and Inchkeith. It's a matter of twenty-nine miles, but those are the names of the islands. That's Inchgarvie there, with the middle pier of the bridge sitting bang on her chest.   She was a fort before Cromwell's time and there's guns on her now.   There's a house that was once a monastery on Inchcolm.   Ye can get there by the wee steamer from Leith. . . .   D'ye see the cranes at Rosyth?   It's a sad place now.   It's all breaking and no building these days.   War-time was the day for Rosyth.   Beatty's fleet went out from there to the Battle of Jutland.   But there's not much but breaking now.   I told you they brought in the old *Tiger* for the smashing, last week.   It's kind o' sad, but . . . Ah, well, it's maybe true what Harry Lauder said."

"And what did he say?"

"Did ye never hear him?   It's in a wee bit patter that goes with one of his songs.   He said: 'It's better to build friendships than battleships.' . . . And there's something in that."

We were certainly so willing to build a friendship with such a pleasant and informative companion that we were scarcely pleased when the ferry-boat, broad and portly as a provost, came sliding up to the pier.

Balaam occupied himself with the slightly tricky business of driving the car aboard, and then the steamer—why do writers persist in calling ferry-boats fussy?—slowly and with dignity glided out into the firth.   And now, as we passed slowly along beside the gigantic red-brown spans, we could see the real size of the Forth Bridge.   Once more a toy train hurried along it, just to oblige us with the comparison.   The frame, which at a distance seems like a delicate tracery, consists of great cylindrical tubes, rather like colossal organ-pipes. The total length, including the end pieces that join the two enormous central spans, is (if you would like to hurl some figures at your friends) one mile 972 yards. As you pass along the whole length you will always reach a point at which the newer, brighter paint reaches the old. There will always be such a point, though it is shifting everyday, because the work of painting goes on continuously, world without end. A Forth Bridge painter must have reached as nearly as is humanly possible the state of perpetual motion. A fellow-passenger on board the boat told us that there were four men whose life-work was dedicated to this service, but I do not know if this is really so. Do these four hypothetical acolytes regard their work as eternally interesting or crushingly monotonous? I should like to know.

We left the boat with a rush after a moment's hesitation, during which I thought that Balaam was going to drive straight into the Firth, and shot up a steep bank which did not, at first sight, appear to lead to anywhere in particular. The Forth Bridge still continued its nonchalant way, stepping lightly over the roofs of the cottages near the pier. We were a little uncertain of our direction and found the signposts slightly confusing, but eventually we decided to let Inverkeithing wait awhile and took the left-hand road for Dunfermline.

The road rose somewhat steeply and Rosyth with

its masts and derricks lay tucked down in the fold
below us. Then, quite suddenly, we saw a city set
on a hill, that could not be hid. It was early evening
when we first saw Dunfermline, but if it looks more
entrancing in any other light, I should be very much
surprised. It was a perfect silhouette, dark yet
luminous, its outline of roofs and towers and slender
spires as sharply edged as if it had been cut with
a knife. The city was on a hill, and outlined against
higher hills. When we reached it and walked along
its steep, narrow streets we found it grey-stoned,
bustling and workaday. Its folk were ordinary folk
like ourselves. But that first glimpse, seen from
the road in that soft, hazy light, showed it to be a
city of dreams. It was, from there, and in that light,
as surely a fairy city as if Merlin, the enchanter, had
raised it from the fold of the hills with a touch of
his wand. So it must have seemed to Saint
Margaret when her royal lover first took her home.
So it must still have seemed in later years when,
riding up from the ferry, she would pause and rest
by the stone that is still called Margaret's Stone.
So, in the magic of a spring evening, it seemed
to us.

We found the place, as I said, real enough, when
we drove in through a sedate new suburb and
climbed the steep street into the town. The streets
were busy and we saw—was not Rosyth but a short
distance away?—many a sailor, walking with his
sweetheart, a heartening sight, for whatever changes

may come to the world, we shall always need sailors, and sailors will always need sweethearts. Another heartening sight to our grateful gaze was a covey of pretty young tram-conductresses, coming off duty with their ticket-boxes under their arms, chattering like happy starlings. An especially interesting feature (as the newspapers say) was the fact that every one of these pretty girls wore her smart peaked cap at what the world has come to know as the Beatty angle. Here was an eloquent tribute to the proximity of Rosyth, and a charming gesture on the part of the lass that loves a sailor. . . .

A policeman, from whom we made some enquiries, was very firm with us. What we wanted to see (whether we knew it or not) was Pittencrieff Glen. "Gifted by Andra Carnegie," he told us. "That's what you'll be wanting to see." Though my first wish was to see, if I could, the place where the king in the ballad sat drinking the bluid-red wine, I did not like to offend the policeman. He said we might take our car along with us if we went in by the coal road, and by the coal road we went.

Pittencrieff Glen is a public park, and something more than a public park. It has its formal part, with neatly laid out flower-beds, lawns, open spaces and bandstands; in short, all that the honest urban mind expects of a public park. But it has another part, which is glen proper, where trees and paths have not been sternly ordered to behave themselves, but where, on the contrary, they ramble up and down the glen-side at their own sweet will, as if they were in the heart of a wooded, hilly countryside and not in the centre of a thriving industrial city. From the terrace in the park we heard the shrill cries of peacocks and in the glen itself there were birds innumerable.

For a long time we watched an elderly gentleman, who was sitting on a seat and crumbling bread out of a paper bag. He was feeding birds, but there was about it nothing of the perfunctory impersonal charity. A little group of bluetits and finches hovered near him and he was trying to see that each one had a fair share. The birds seemed to have alternate fits of boldness and shyness. They would swoop down from their branches and flutter back again, but each time they flew down, they would come a little nearer until they were in reach of their benefactor's hand, and, having pecked quietly at their portion of bread, flew swiftly away again. So the hungry were fed, until they had all had their share, except one especially shy little bluetit, which kept hopping wistfully about but could not bring himself to the point of coming nearer. The man with the bread addressed him solemnly.

"Come awa', come awa', ma bonnie wee boy. Ye're the only yin that hasn't had his piece. Och, ye wee gowk"—this as the bird fluttered back on to the tree again—"as if I would hurt ye! Come awa', come awa', ma bonnie boy."

So, with infinite patience and solemn cajolery,

he succeeded in prevailing on the last bluetit to come and have his "piece."

If you go up through the Glen this way you will come to the ruins of the old Palace. This undoubtedly was the place where the bluid-red wine was drunk, but the ruins are rather small. You seem to be looking down on a cross-section of the kitchen premises, and it is rather disappointing, when you have been thinking of a banqueting-hall, celebrated in the noblest of ballads, to see little more than the cellars from which the bluid-red wine was brought.

Even if little remains, the Palace has a tale of history that few, if any, Scottish buildings can equal, for it was a royal residence long before Edinburgh gained any importance. The great Malcolm built it. It may be that he brought his bride to this palace when he brought her home from shipwreck on the Firth, but it is more likely that he built it afterwards in her honour. The mound on which his first Tower was raised still stands in the curving loop of the burn at the lower end of the glen. Indeed they say that this was the first Dunfermline —the fort of the fiar (crooked) linn. The sons and daughter of Malcolm and Margaret were born here; Edgar, Alexander and David and Maud, who married the Norman Henry the First. When Edward the First invaded Scotland for the second time, he held his court here and thoughtfully set it on fire when he left it. James the Fourth, the brave king who died at Flodden, re-built it, and afterwards it was linked with the sad story of the house of Stuart. Mary, Queen of Scots, lived here for awhile. Her son here signed the Covenant and his son Charles I here began an ill-fated life. So many of the Stuart sorrows are linked with this once grand palace of which little more than the cellars remain.

As you come out of the Glen at this point you find yourself facing the steps, the tower and the western doorway of Dunfermline Abbey. The Abbey, like the glen, has an older and a newer part. The old part is Norman and magnificent; the other is neither Norman nor, in my opinion, magnificent. It is large and is executed in what my guide-book —sometimes I suspect a satirical vein in that incomparable volume—describes as the style of 1817–22. On the top of the high tower rests a stone balustrading which consists of the words, King Robert the Bruce, carved in huge letters, a word to each side of the square. This feat of sculpture was no doubt nobly intentioned, but it is not very beautiful, though it scarcely deserved Balaam's graceless comment that the people who did that sort of thing did so much better in butter.

The lovely older part is not the church originally founded and built by Malcolm and Margaret. Their son, David the First, replaced their church by the one of which the beautiful nave remains. The Lady chapel in which the good queen and her lord were buried, has gone, but the tombs remain in what is now a gracious churchyard.

In the new church sleeps Scotland's greatest king.
His brave heart, as everyone knows, rests, after
strange adventures, at Melrose Abbey, but his body
lies here. When Burns visited Dunfermline, he
knelt and kissed the two broad flagstones which
marked the grave of Bruce in the churchyard and
cursed "the worse than Gothic neglect of the first
of Scottish heroes." Now that neglect has been
remedied and faithfully atoned. When they were
digging out the foundations of the new church they
found the body, sealed in two leaden caskets and
wound in a shroud of golden thread. Now the
body, newly coffined, lies beneath the pulpit.

A king, a man, a heroic legend; most romantic
of fugitives, for he spent much of his life in hiding
from implacable enemies; doughtiest of warriors, for
all the old tales tell how he fought against incredible
odds with his own sword in his own hand; matchless
leader of men, for he made a great, proud nation
from a handful of sullen, dispirited and broken clans.
He never called his men to a fight, where he did not
go first, risking death a thousand times, in pitched
battle or wayside skirmish. Men will sometimes
judge greatness by victories in war, but the triumph
of Bannockburn was but the pennon on his spear,
compared to the real greatness of the man. That
greatness was not his military prowess in victory,
but his deathless courage in defeat after defeat.
Bruce and the spider . . . a tale told by smug
Victorian parents to spur their offspring on to deeds

of derring-do in the counting-house. And yet . . .
the tale is true. God has given to man certain gifts
that may distinguish him from the beasts that
perish; the gifts of laughter, of pity, of the love of
lovely things; but more godlike than all, for without
it the others cannot live, is the gift of courage, to
strive, to seek, to find and not to yield. And in
that gift of unquenchable courage God was more
generous to Robert the Bruce than to any man who
ever lived. . . .

*　　　*　　　*　　　*　　　*

Musing on this as we came down the Abbey steps,
we had need of something to bring us back to a
workaday world. And we found it. At the foot
of the steps, we saw a curious horsedrawn cart,
which bore the mystic legend, CHIPPER. Not roast
chestnuts or pea-nuts, but chipped potatoes, all, so
to speak, a-growing and a-blowing. A very sharp
reminder, indeed, of this interesting modern world,
but nothing to break the heart over, for as Doctor
Johnson said, and said truly when he came away
from the sacred ruins of St. Andrews: "Ay, ay,
amidst all these sorrowful scenes, I have no objection
to dinner."

Ay, ay, but not from an itinerant chipper.

IV

"I'M AWA' TO FIFE!"

THE coast of Fife is the Breezy Coast in little.
People who come from Fife will tell you that
they come from the Kingdom, as who should say:
"We belong to something entirely separate and
infinitely superior. No connection with the other
person (or persons) over the way." I am a Tweed-
side man myself and, speaking purely as a Borderer,
I am not prepared to admit the Fifers' claims of
complete superiority, but, speaking in a general way
and to an English audience, it might be conceded
that the Fifers have a certain right to their separation
and a just cause for pride in their Kingdom.

The Kingdom has the right to be regarded
separately, because of its shape; a compact and self-
contained peninsula between the deep indentations
of the Firths of Forth and Tay. This habit of
being self-contained is Fifeshire's strongest characteristic, a trait which it has imparted to the little
fishing towns that dot its breezy coast and to its
inhabitants themselves. The queer old-fashioned
little towns, once bustling and now picturesquely
quiet, are self-contained. So are the fisher-folk
and others who live there.

In what way Fife was a Kingdom, as distinguished
from the rest of Scotland, is not quite clear to me.
Perhaps it was so called because it contained in
those earliest days the old capital of the Picts; per-

haps because, on account of its position and resources, it could afford to be self-supporting and independent. (It was never part of the Roman province of Britain.) But your loyal Fifer has no doubt that the real reason was that Fife was Fife, and no intelligent person would be interested in inferior localities.

James the First—England's James the First—was the last person I should have suspected of poetic leanings, yet he coined a romantic phrase which is as true as it is happy. "Fife," he said, "is a grey cloth mantle with a golden fringe." That was well said, and, though we were not lacking in respect for the grey cloth mantle, we were more disposed to take delight in the golden fringe. There is no doubt about the golden quality. The sand of innumerable little bays and coves is golden. So is the sunshine that kisses the shore. It is no drowsy or sweltering sun that shines there, for Fife is no Lotus-land, but a sunlight that brings life and vigour, dancing through the crisp salty air upon waves and golden shore.

That especial salty crispness in the Fife air is very important. You find it not only in the atmosphere but in the character of the people. It is not merely that so many of them are sailors or fishermen. There is in their attitude to life and in their everyday talk a peculiar dry and salty flavour, a certain knowingness and a quiet self-satisfaction that is not in the least offensive to the

65   E

stranger. Their knowingness has nothing of the egregious cleverness of the modern "smart Alec"; it is—using the word in its old-fashioned Elizabethan sense—a humour, and a delightful humour, too. Naturally a Fifer takes a quiet pleasure in knowing what's what, but he does not necessarily despise you for your ignorance of that knowledge.

If you see a Fife fisherman, sitting beside an upturned boat and smoking a cutty pipe with peculiar zest in the smoking, you may find him rather difficult to engage in conversation. If he consents to talk to you, he will talk courteously and with an air of philosophy. You will know at once that you are not talking to an ignoramus. Fife lairds, it was once said, were known by the salt water on their hats, and your Fife fisherman is known by his salty humour.

If he tells you that the fishing is bad, he is genuinely lamenting old times when each little burgh on the Fife coast, with its nets and its doo-cots, was bustling and prosperous; he is sad for the plight of a fine and brave industry. But he is not making a fuss over the fact that he himself has been having a particularly bad time. Though troubles may come, they have to be weathered as the fishing-boat weathers the gales, and there is no sense in worrying over troubles that have not yet arrived.

"I'll no tak' off my breeks," he will say, "till I gang to bed."

And even when troubles do arrive he is disposed to be thankful that they are no worse.

"Better half an egg," he will tell you, "than a toom doup."

That is the sort of man who is facing the hard times of to-day with a wry, but brave, smile and that salty twinkle of the eye. He will not argue with you if you criticise Fife. Sad to relate, there have been people who have dared to criticise the Fifers, and their saucy comments have come down proverbially. There is a poem which begins: "I never likit the Kingdom of Fife," and another which contains the line: "There's silly-daft folk in Fife." Much Fife cares, even when Fifish intelligence is questioned. It was once said that a Fifer was known by four things—"a puckle land, a lump of debt, a doo-cot and a law plea." And Baroness Nairne once wrote a mischievous, rollicking song:

Ye shouldna' ca' the laird daft, daftlike though he may be;
Ye shouldna' ca' the laird daft, he's just as wise as we;
Ye shouldna ca' the laird daft, his bonnet has a bee,
H e's just a wee bit *Fifish*, like some Fife lairds that be.

But when you repeat to your good Fifer such atrocious libels as this, he will only shrug his shoulders. If people must say such foolish things as this, why then, they must. Nothing will stop them. "Wha will to Cupar," he says, shaking his head, "maun to Cupar." But in the end his eye will still have that salty twinkle, which suggests that probably the

67

best stories against Fife are made up by the Fifers themselves.

I once knew a lady whose duty it was to "do for" a Fife minister, who was "a wee bit Fifish." He was a scholar, a gentleman and more than half a saint, but his other-worldliness was a sore trial to the good lady who had him in her care. New clothes were an abomination to him and no power on earth would induce him to enter a tailor's, so that when a pair of trousers began to wear out, dire consequences were threatened. "I could make the legs," said his housekeeper, "but further than that was beyond me, so I had to sew a pair of black legs to his old ones. Many's the time he's been up to the Assembly at Edinburgh, with nothing but a frock-coat to hide what I'd done for him. A fine man, but. . . . *Fifish.*"

From Dunfermline we made our way back to the Firth as quickly as possible, for the hurried traveller must naturally prefer the gold fringe to the grey mantle. It was as we were coming down to Aberdour that a small boy made a determined attempt to commit *hari-kiri* beneath our wheels. Balaam pulled up like lightning and the young would-be suicide went his way, smiling. I mention the lad, not in criticism of his determined habit of playing on a main road, but as a point of interest. He was bowling along, not a hoop, but a motor-tyre. This use of a tyre, while it marks another step in the relentless march of progress, makes life a little more difficult for the motorist. It is dangerous for a small boy to run suddenly across the road with a hoop. It is even worse with a large tyre. Still, at no time in the world's history was it ever worth while arguing with the young. Youth, progress, and motor-tyres *will* be served. . . .

Inverkeithing has a fine wide main street and a general air of wishing to look up-to-date and not quite managing it. The burgh need not be ashamed of its old houses with their tiled roofs, which are handsomer than what people build now. The church, the old tower of which is very fine, is famous, not only as an ancient ecclesiastical building, but as containing one of the few old fonts left in Presbyterian churches. It is strange that such a Popish thing—it is supported by extremely papistical angels—should have escaped the furies of the image-breaking Reformers, but now it rests in peace and a kindlier age has restored it to its rightful home.

The most famous house in Inverkeithing is near the church. It was once, they say, the palace of Arabella Drummond, the beautiful queen of Robert the Third. This poor lady must have had great sadness in her life, for her eldest son, the Duke of Rothesay, was the victim of one of the foulest murders in history. Scott's *Fair Maid of Perth* gives an enthralling picture of these troublous times. Through the sinister plottings of his uncle, the Duke of Albany, young Rothesay was flung into a

69

dungeon at Falkland Castle and allowed slowly to starve to death. His gaolers, with a callousness rare even in those brutal days, watched him dying of hunger day by day. Two peasant women, hearing his tortured cries, made brave efforts to give him food. One brought barley scones concealed under her veil and another gave him milk from her own breast. Their sweet charity was of no avail, for they were caught and driven away. The young duke died in horrible agony. . . . The evils that befell Scotland in the following years were looked on as God's punishment for this dreadful crime. A sad house must have been this queen's palace, looking out on to the grey Firth.

The road to Aberdour does not go so closely down to the shore as does most of Fife's coast-roads. Between Inverkeithing and Dalgety Bay lie the remains of Donibristle House, where another ghastly deed was done. It would seem to be a house of evil, for three times it has been burned, and has not been really restored. The evil deed was the murder, told in one of the most vivid and moving of the old Scots ballads, of the Bonnie Earl of Moray. It was in the dark days at the end of the sixteenth century, when every man's hand was against another's, and when Scotland was so full of treasons, stratagems and spoils that a man could not trust his brother or his best friend.

Moray was young, brave, handsome, and, as a leader of the Protestant cause, popular with a hero-worshipping people. Whether his murder was the result of a clan-feud or egged on by political animosity will never be known. But his enemies carried out their plot with fierce ruthlessness. They crossed the Queen's Ferry, and coming upon Moray with his tutor, the brave Sheriff Dunbar, in lonely Donibristle, set fire to the house. Caught like rats in a trap, the two had the alternative of being burnt alive or making a wild despairing dash for the open.

"Let me go first," cried the brave Dunbar. "Mistaking me for your lordship in the mirk of the night, they will set on me, and that will give you a chance to escape."

Dunbar rushed out and went down, fighting desperately, under a dozen stabbing poniards. Moray slipped by in the darkness and sped to the shore, but a gold string upon his "cnap-scull tippet" which had caught fire, lit a flaming path and his relentless foes saw where he was. In another moment they were upon him, stabbing and hacking. As he fell bleeding among the rocks, Huntley, his chief enemy, slashed at his dying face with cruel dagger. There was a matchless stoic courage in Moray's last gasp:

"Ah," said he, "you have spoiled a better face than your ain."

And still, over the gaunt remains of Donibristle, hangs the shadow of an evil deed. . . .

Aberdour is another of those small places which

try to forget their ancient history by being bright, up-to-date seaside resorts. It has a beautiful little bay and once boasted a Pilgrims' Well, which brought healing to sore eyes. It has a ruined castle, too, standing gaunt and windswept above the Dourburn. Here fled, at the time of his fall from power, the greedy and Machiavellian Regent Morton, evil genius of an evil age, and inventor of that primitive guillotine called the Maiden, by whose knife he was the first to fall. (Or so says legend, ever a lover of poetic justice.) During his days of power, he was relentless in his avarice, and, like an English Morton, found many devious ways of wringing gold from the people, and it is said that, in his last fears before capture, he hid his vast treasure under the stone in front of the castle gateway. But wherever he hid it, he performed the task with that cunning which was his chief trait, for no one has found it yet. . . .

After leaving Aberdour, we came along a high marine drive, from which the land below slopes steeply to the water. Here is seen what surely must be the most stupendous view of the Firth. It is rather like one of those photographs which the camera-man takes in sections and pieces together afterwards, so that the finished picture will stretch along one wall of your house. We saw the picture, too, in the soft evening light, as, by sheer good luck, we had already seen more than one fine picture— and the southern shore of the Firth at that hour was "the scenery of a fairy dream." The far-famed reek of Edinburgh was no reek at all but rather an enchanted mist, whence rose the pinnacles and minarets of a fairy city, which seemed to rest, not on solid earth, but on a magic cloudland. There was the Forth Bridge, far on the right, its metalwork a delicate tracery. There was Arthur's Seat —a seat that Merlin had conjured for his royal master. The whole city was so tinged with softened splendour that it seemed for a moment to have no place upon a sordid earth. Dunfermline had been wonderful in this light but Edinburgh was even lovelier. When Boswell said that the Firth of Forth was finer than the prospect from Constantinople or the bay of Naples, Johnson poohpoohed the claim. "Ay," he said, "that is the state of the world. Water is the same everywhere." But that was only the Grand Cham's fun. Besides, he did not see the prospect from the road to Burntisland on a golden evening.

Inchcolm, which we saw in the Firth, has a history, which might have been tranquil and peaceful, but, unhappily, was not. Alexander the First founded a monastery there early in the twelfth century, but the bare, mysterious island was inhabited before the coming of Christianity, for it was once called the Druids' Isle. It seems, also, from earliest times, to have been a base for the old Norse pirates. A holy hermit—his cell remains to this day—once lived there and sheltered King

Alexander in a storm which drove him ashore. It was in thankfulness for the anchorite's kindly, if Spartan, welcome, that the King founded the monastery which, by subsequent endowments, became very rich. Its wealth was its misfortune, for it made the island monastery a temptation and an easy prey to later generations of sea-rovers and to the English, to whom war and piracy, in troubled times, were all one. It was said God punished the invaders by tempests and plagues for their sacrilege, but the evil was done, for the island became, instead of a holy place, once more a pirates' lair and then a refuge for the plague-stricken. During the War, the island was fortified and the abbey tower was used as an observation post.

The other inch which we could see ahead has a tall lighthouse, and is manned by guns that guard the Firth entrance. That brave king who died at Flodden once made a strange attempt to discover the primitive speech of mankind. On the conveniently lonely island of Inchkeith, he had two small children, boy and girl, brought up under the care of a good woman who was dumb, the King's theory being that, hearing no human tongue, they would begin to speak by the light of nature. The result of this pleasant philosophical-cum-philological experiment is recorded by one chronicler:

"Some say," he begins, with all the excitement of a piece of hot journalism, "that 'they spak very guid Ebrew'." But just as he has raised our interest, he stamps it down again, by adding: "But, for myself, I know not." What language did they speak, if any?

"If the experiment were undertaken now," said Balaam, "there is no doubt that the twins would speak Chicago American, which is indubitably and unhappily the universal language of our own day."

After the Battle of Pinkie the English captured and fortified the island, and in the religious war that followed it had a French garrison. To this day, it is an island fort.

A pleasant interlude of comedy in the island's stern warlike history was the visit of Dr. Johnson on his Scottish tour. The Doctor insisted on visiting the island, though landing was difficult and they had to clamber up a very steep ascent. He was in great form, mercilessly "ragging" poor Boswell all the time. "He stalked like a giant among the luxuriant thistles and nettles" and, no doubt, congratulated Bozzy upon this typically Scottish vegetation. He quizzed Boswell about a certain type of travel-book, in a satirical manner which makes at least one writer feel guilty of having written travel-books at all.

"He bade me," says Boswell, "try to write a description of our discovering Inch Keith, in the usual style of travellers, describing fully every particular; stating grounds on which we concluded that it must have been once inhabited, and introducing many sage reflections, and we should see how a thing might be covered in words, so as to induce people to come and survey it. All that was told might be true and yet in reality there might be nothing to see."

And when I read this passage to Balaam, as we stood on the high road looking down on the Firth, he laughed wickedly.

"Your usual method," said he, "and the method of all your tribe."

Unkind, and if true of me, entirely untrue of my betters; but even if every writer of travel-books were to be shot at dawn, I would swear this: that if a man came from London to Scotland and saw nothing but the picture of the Firth with that soft "reekie" silhouette of dreaming spires beyond, he would have made a profitable and worth-while journey.

Burntisland is the town to which, if we had not been so anxious to sail alongside the Forth Bridge, we might have come by ferry from Granton, thereby shortening our journey. It has history enough for any ten towns, and, besides being a pleasure resort, still retains a certain bustle of trading which many of the Fife coast towns have lost. You will see the coal-boats in the harbour, which has been built in what must have been a splendid natural position long before coal-boats were thought of. Even in the days of the earliest Roman invaders it was looked on as an ideal trading port.

When Cromwell would have stormed it, in the

time of the Battle of Dunbar, the town voluntarily surrendered in exchange for the invaders' promise to pave its streets, repair its harbour, and strengthen the fortifications of the commanding slopes behind. Surely this was the most intelligent policy ever pursued by a beleaguered garrison, for Cromwell, who did things solidly or not at all, kept his part of the bargain and built more strongly than had ever been built before.

Rossend Castle looks down on the harbour on one side and a little bay on the other; its gaze is not so grim as that of so many castles that look out to sea. Something of the beauty and sadness of a tragic queen remains with ivy-clad Rossend, and when Johnson said there were only two trees in Fife, he lied, for there are here many old and gracious trees which must have been a-growing in the old curmudgeon's time.

A Durie of Durie built the place in the fourteen hundreds, and for long it was a seaside resort of the abbots of Dunfermline. (Many of the famous Duries were abbots; as, indeed, Duries were everything of note.) The oldest Rossend story concerns the relics of Queen Margaret—the skull adorned with jewels and (more strangely) with flowing auburn hair. In the image-breaking days of the Reformation, these sacred relics were in grave danger, but a brave abbot—also a Durie—rescued them and brought them, by way of Edinburgh, to Rossend.

Where are they now? A sight of that flowing auburn hair might have converted many a sceptic to a belief in miracles. Alas, the relics are no longer at Rossend. Near the end of the eighteenth century they were in the Jesuit College at Douai, but when revolutions break out it is a sad time for royal jewels, whether they be holy relics or not. So no one now living has seen those auburn tresses. . . .

Cromwell had his headquarters here and, true to his honest bargain, did the castle no harm, but a romantic eye will look further back than Cromwell to a time when, in a queen's bedroom, a poet, mad for love, committed an act of immortal folly for which the penalty was the gallows.

The beauty of Mary Queen of Scots drew service and devotion as a magnet draws steel. But it was the madness of the young French poet Chastelard not that he should die, fighting for her in battle, but that he should give himself to certain disgrace and death for the sake of a moment alone with her. Never did youth love so blindly or insanely. He was a courtier, trained in the school of ancient chivalry and a poet trained in the school of the master, Ronsard. He loved the queen so madly that he hid in her room and was discovered there by her maids of honour. It was an unpardonable offence, but it gained pardon . . . once. Her beautiful eyes bewitched him once more. The madness came on him again. For a second time he hid in her room. This time there could be no pardon. His criminal folly brought him to the scaffold, yet he faced death as might a soldier and a poet. On the scaffold he turned in the direction of the queen's window and cried out: *"Adieu, toi si belle et si cruelle, qui me tues et que je ne puis cesser d'aimer."* There may be few that died for love, but Pierre de Chastelard was one.

From Burntisland we ran along a low road with high, steep banks above us on our left and a bright expanse of golden sand stretching away to the far water upon our right. By the roadside stands a slender obelisk commemorating the untimely end of King Alexander the Third. He was a wise and kindly king and "virtuous in governing." Returning from a royal banquet in Edinburgh, he made his way to the ferry amid howling wind and blinding rain. His followers begged him to stay safely ashore and not brave the darkness of gale and flood. A disastrous storm was portended, and Thomas the Rhymer of Ercildoune had foretold a storm that would rage unchecked from Ross to the Solway. But the king would heed the advice of neither bard, noble, nor ferry-man. He "ettled" to be home, to his newly-wedded queen, who lay at Kinghorn Castle. The ferry-man, in loyalty, gave way. "Go will I," said he at last, "for if I must die, I will die with my king."

But he was not to die with his king, for the boat, though tossed by the tempest, reached the Fife shore in safety. There the storm grew even wilder, but nothing would stay the king. It was as if some madness possessed him. Mounting his horse, he pressed on through the mirk of the storm. His terrified retinue followed him along the rough path at the cliff's edge. Only their horses could guide them, for the night was black as pitch. Suddenly the nearest attendant heard the sound of a horse stumbling. A wild cry rang out.

"My lord the king!" he shouted in an agony of fear. But the only answer was the skirl of the wind and the beating of the waves. The king had fallen to his death. When the morning sun rose over calm blue water, there were those who, not knowing that the king lay dead, mocked at the prophecy of True Thomas. But with the death of the king a storm had burst which was to plunge Scotland to disaster, for the heir to the throne was a slip of a girl and already greedy hands were stretched out to snatch the crown. Scotland was to know no peace from that evil storm until Bruce should bravely bring it.

Kinghorn Castle, where Alexander's queen waited sadly for her lord, no longer stands, nor do the Glamis Tower and St. Leonard's Chapel. Johnson and Boswell dined here after their amusing exploration of Inchkeith, but did not stay long, hurrying off by post-chaise to Cupar, where the Doctor, after Boswell's attempt to "scottify" his palate, was glad to take a dish of his well-loved tea.

"Burntisland for salted herring," says the old proverb.

"And Kinghorn for cursing and swearing. . . ."

We heard no swearing in the narrow but perfectly respectable streets. No doubt the label came from sterner times when Kinghorn fishermen and their womenfolk, too, had a special genius for speaking their mind. Many men from the Fife coast were in the Covenanting army which was routed by Montrose at Kilsyth, and the womenfolk of Kinghorn especially cursed the fanatical war-preachers who, they said, had taken away their husbands and sons and left the town "full of faitherless bairns." Kilsyth left a terrible scar upon Fife and may well have given Fifers of a later day something of a distaste for active religious controversy.

And now in the distance we could see the smoke of a myriad tall chimneys. We were approaching Kirkcaldy, and as Kirkcaldy is a long town—indeed, it is *the* Lang Toun—it at least deserves to start its length upon a new page.

V

THE LANG TOUN AND ONWARDS

KIRKCALDY is famous for Adam Smith and oil-cloth. It also has the longest main street in Scotland and has a pleasantly humorous habit of making jokes about (and against) itself. Except for its long sands, it is not beautiful enough for the traveller to say that it wears a smiling face; he might say, rather, that the town wears a good-natured grin, for Kirkcaldy has a peculiarly (and pleasantly) Fifish way with it. It has a sly, pawky way of looking out on life—slow in speech, but rich in implication—which is the epitome of Fifish character. Carlyle said of the Kirkcaldy folk that they were "a pleasant, honest kind of fellow-mortals; something of quietly fruitful, of good *old Scotch* in their works and ways; more vernacular, peaceable, fixed and almost genial in their mode of life, than I had been used to in the Border homeland." *Almost genial* . . . A marvellous phrase, that, and, coming from where it did, doubly ironical.

There is an old local saw: "They say the deil's deid and buried in Kirkcaldy." Personally, the world being what it is to-day, I might have taken leave to doubt this, but the Kirkcaldy folk will produce for your benefit evidence that cannot lightly be gainsaid. They will show you at Balwearie the enormous wall of the Wizard's tower, where lived an old acquaintance of ours, Michael Scott, who has kept continually cropping up in our travels. If anyone was capable of dealing faithfully with the devil it was Michael. The devil called on Michael for the purpose of carrying him off, but seems to have had so much the worse of the argument as to find himself committed to the performance of three impossible tasks. This was Michael's favourite ploy with fiends—he bamboozled an innocent demon in the same way when he lived at Melrose—and one wonders how any fiend could have been so simple-minded as to undertake the tasks, the last of which was to twine a rope out of the sands of Kirkcaldy Bay. The poor devil (poor devil) went on working with the dank, slippery sand and finally succumbed, as well he might, to an attack of cold feet. "Ma taes are cauld!" he wailed pathetically, and that, I take it, was the end of him. If this story is true, then it may be taken as unimpeachable evidence that the deil is dead and buried in Kirkcaldy.

The long main street of Kirkcaldy almost fulfils the geometrical definition of a straight line, having length and scarcely any breadth, and the little streets and wynds that run into it are narrower still. We saw on our left hand a Fish Wynd and Flesh Wynd, romantic reminder of the days when streets were known by the name of the goods they sold. Adam Smith, "Kirkcaldy's most famous son," was born in Kirkgate and came back, after an astonishing academic career, to write *The Wealth of Nations* in a little house in the High Street. He must have been a man of simply devastating learning, and while the modern world may not be grateful to him for being so tremendous a pioneer of "the dismal science," it is unquestionably to his credit that he was among that band of scholars who were kind to Robert Burns when he rode into Edinburgh on Rosinante.

It is said that, when a little boy, he was kidnapped and carried off by tinkers, and there are those who assert that his theory of political economy, which held the field for over a hundred years, has recently fallen among thieves. Young Adam escaped from the tinkers and perhaps his economic theories may come into their own again. And perhaps not. Those who believe that the nineteenth century represented the highest peak of human endeavour, must thank Adam Smith, for on the economic theories that he enunciated its whole fabric indubitably rested. On the other hand, those who loathe the industrial age and all that it stood for, may reasonably heave their brickbats in his direction. Either way, he cannot be ignored. He was a very big man.

Another famous son of Kirkcaldy, not, perhaps, so distinguished as Adam Smith but a man of high importance, was Michael Nairn, the romantically-minded manufacturer who invented oilcloth. However stirring Kirkcaldy's ancient history may have been, it was Nairn who put modern Kirkcaldy on the map. And perhaps there is something solemn and grand in having produced an article which is to be

found to-day wherever civilised feet have stood. It
is an achievement, at any rate, not lightly to be
despised. Balaam expressed himself a great admirer
of Michael Nairn, and of his persistent faith in a
new idea which the pundits pooh-poohed, as they
always do. (There never was yet a practical idea in
this world at which the practical people did not
jeer.)

"I'd like to have met Mr. Nairn," said Balaam,
"partly to tell him that I admire oilcloth as a floor-
covering, but partly to ask him what there is about
it which conduces to petty crime. If you live in
the country, you will always be pestered by vaga-
bonds who want to sell you something at the door,
and the most persistent scoundrels are the vendors of
odd lengths of oilcloth. They will wear green baize
aprons and say it was left over from a job at Lord
What's-his-name's. Or they will wear sailors' caps
and say it is the last of their cargo. Let a man be
scoundrel, if he will. But why is it always oilcloth?"

Why? I do not know, but I am certain it is not
Michael Nairn's fault.

The smoke of Kirkcaldy's chimneys will never
spoil Kirkcaldy's sands. Carlyle, who with Irving,
his friend and rival for the hand of Jane Welch,
taught school at Kirkcaldy, spoke of summer twilight
on the beach in one of his lightning-flash descrip-
tions.

"A mile of the smoothest sand, with one long

85

wave coming on gently, steadily, and breaking in gradual explosion into harmless white, the break of it melodiously rushing along like a mane of foam, beautifully sounding, and advancing from the West Burn to the Harbour."

Here are the phrases of a poet. "Gradual explosion . . . melodiously rushing . . . a mane of foam." These came not from the Sage of Chelsea nor from the thrawn dyspeptic of Craigenputtock, but from the heart of a young man in love, "melodiously rushing along."

Edward Irving, too, saw truth and beauty from Kirkcaldy Sands and would take his pupils out there on still nights and bid them watch the stars.

One of the most richly human characters who ever walked the sands was the old minister, Robert Shirra, who prayed and preached near the end of the eighteenth century. Shirra was undoubtedly "a wee bit Fifish," and some of his queer sayings and doings are still told of with a chuckle. Of the outlandish new doctrine of the Equality of Man he said that it was against the course of Nature, and that he had never met it in his travels, on earth, in heaven, or in hell. Yet though, like many a good man, he railed against equality in theory, he practised it contentedly, living among his fisher-flock like a true fisher of men. When it was rumoured that they might expect a raid from that debonair pirate, Paul Jones, Shirra led his congregation down on to the sands and, all kneeling, prayed for nice, good roaring gales to blow the privateer, if not to the bottom of the sea, at least backwards out of the Firth. And the pawky prayer was answered, for Paul Jones never landed at Kirkcaldy. The privateersmen, so the tale runs, saw the red shawls of the kneeling fish-wives and thought them the scarlet jackets of the king's men, preparing a warm welcome for the invaders. So Paul Jones, without waiting for the contrary winds of heaven, showed Fife a clean pair of heels. Another tale told of Shirra is that when he read out from the pulpit the Psalmist's observation on the mendacity of the human race, he paused and then added: "Ay, Dauvit, and had ye lived in the Lang Toun, ye micht hae said it at your leesure!"

We made our way, still steadily along the coast, under Pathhead, towards Dysart. The upstanding but roofless pile on the hill is Ravenscraig Castle, a good name for such a place. It was designed by James the Second and built by his widow, Mary of Gueldres, coming afterwards into the hands of the St. Clairs of Roslin. Scott tells of this castle in his tale of Rosabelle.

There were wooded slopes on our left as we followed the winding way to Dysart, and here we saw more trees, in their first gracious spring green, than we had seen before. This wooded hillside finally disposed of Dr. Johnson's little joke that there were only two trees in Fife. We had never quite believed it. He made a similar joke, you will remember, about the timber on the Isle of Mull, which, he said, had been largely increased because he left a good walking-stick there. All through his journey to Fife he was in especially good form, never ceasing to pull Boswell's leg the whole time. When he saw one or two peasants wearing shoes he put down this sign of prosperity as a result of the Union with England, for it was common knowledge, he said, "that you all went barefoot before." "Don't talk to me of your great lairds," he said, "for anyone in Scotland who possesses a two-horse-cart is somebody. . . ."

Dysart sounds romantic enough to have derived from something better than the ordinary Latin word *desertum*, which referred to the lonely cave of St. Serf upon the sea-shore. All the Fife burghs were famous for something, as the old rhyme will tell you:

> Dysart for coal and sault,
> Pathhead for meal and mault,
> Kirkcaldy for lasses braw,
> Kinghorn for breaking the law.

From which it will be seen that the rhyming epigrammatist had been hurrying along the coast in the opposite direction to our own. Besides coal—we saw miners on the roads with lamps hanging from their caps—and salt, Dysart was noted for its canty carles.

("What *are* carles?" asked Balaam.)

Carles were, and are, I suppose, the jolly lads of the village, which local patriotism has a perfect right to praise as being finer fellows than their neighbours. Did not Burns himself honour them with a song?

> Up with the carls o' Dysart
> And the lads o' Buckhaven,
> And the Kimmers o' Largo,
> And the lasses o' Leven.

But the carles came first. . . .

Dysart is queer, rambling and old, and its flax-works and coal-trade have not succeeded in destroying its flavour of age. The haven is old, rocky and weather-beaten, and near to it is the ruined ivy-clad church of St. Serf. The cave where this early saint fled from the busy world and wrestled alone with the Prince of Darkness has been made into an oratory.

All along the Fife coast you will see evidence of what architects call "Dutch influence," and you will see this more in Dysart than anywhere else. Dysart has been called "Little Holland," and I suppose much of its old trade must have been with the Dutch when they were one of the great seafaring nations. Many of the houses near the quay and the Town Hall above might have come from some queer little Dutch town. Here we see Dutch quaintness and also Dutch cleanliness. It is not strange to discover things Dutch on this East Coast, for you will find a Holland in Lincolnshire and a Little Holland in Essex. Probably the Dutch, except in Van Tromp's time, did us less harm than any of our neigh-bours. . . .

The coast here is full of rambling caves which, no doubt, were the haunts of smugglers in the old days, for the Dutch were great shippers of spirits and tobacco, and few folk in Fife, or, indeed, anywhere else in Scotland, thought it morally wrong to get the better of the Revenue. The deil might well fly awa' wi' the Exciseman, for all the canty carles of Dysart cared.

Wemyss—there is an East and a West Wemyss— is especially famous for its caves, but we had no leisure to visit them, as our road turned from sight of the sea and we hurried along through an industrial patch, where we again saw miners with lamps in their caps. One of the caves is called the Glass Cave and here the early glass-workers made their first windows and, satisfying an even stronger human need, their first bottles.

Wemyss Castle stands on a high cliff with trees around it; but although Macduff was the first "lord of Wemyss," that is, of the caves, the ruin that is called Macduff's Castle lies farther along the coast towards Buckhaven. Wemyss Castle has a long history and its best-known story tells of the meeting of Mary Queen of Scots with her cousin, Darnley.

It is possible that they may have met previously when Darnley was sent by his ambitious mother to visit the French court, but it was at Wemyss that they were first really thrown together.

("Ah," said Chastelard, "you like better that lang lad.") At least she liked the lang lad well enough to marry him, and no doubt he was a handsome, burly fellow then. How long did she like him? As long, at least, as they were at Wemyss, for times were gay; there was hawking and hunting, and the feasting and entertainment were so elaborate as to impoverish the not very wealthy countryside.

No one knows, and no one will ever know, the true tale of Mary and Darnley. At first he was kind in in his rough and uncouth way. Afterwards he was a brute, though never such a brute as Bothwell. For long afterwards Mary's complicity in his murder was taken for granted, but such of the evidence as was not circumstantial, was in the hands of unscrupulous enemies. The assumption of her guilt was part of sinister policy. Much of that evidence, once treated as unassailable fact, has crumbled. Nothing that we now know for certain can diminish our pity for the tragic queen, so brave, so friendless and, in all real respects, so utterly lonely. With the lang lad's mysterious death, she exchanged a bad husband for a worse, and for that step, whether it was folly or worse than folly, she paid in sorrow a hundredfold.

Buckhaven, once famed for its merry lads, is sober and quiet enough now, an old-fashioned fishing village of the old Fifish kind. Here is the old type of fisherman, slow of speech and very laconic. Fifers from other burghs speak knowingly of the College of Buckhaven, but this place of learning is in the same category as the sea-coast of Bohemia or the far-famed Wigan Pier. "There ain't no sich place." It was explained to me by a Fifeshire friend as the spot where "a body that never kent onything learned all he ever kent." It was, I think, from Dubbieside, the old course near Buckhaven, that the story of the two laconic golfers first came. They had gone round the course, battling their way through the bunkers in grimly silent antagonism. On the last tee, Sandy broke the oppressive silence.

"Dormy," he said, venturing the first remark of the day.

Donald turned on him in furious indignation.

"Chatterbox!" he roared and stalked disgustedly to the clubhouse.

In Fifeshire there is a shortage of surnames and, in Buckhaven especially, surnames are a luxury, so that a man there, I have been told, is either called Thomson or by the name of his wife, as it might be, Meg's Sandy or Ailie's Jock. And perhaps from Buckhaven sprang that great ethnological theory which tells us that we're a' Jock Tamson's bairns. . . .

Leven has large spinning works and an export trade in coal, but industry has not spoiled its reputation as a health resort, and nothing can spoil its fine sands. They stretch along eastwards as far as eye can see, towards Lundin Links, where there is golf, *par excellence*.

I can imagine nothing more exhilarating than to drive out along this coast-road on a spring morning. There was a fresh breeze from the sea, keen, clean and heartening. Sunlight gleamed back from sand and sea, and even the clouds in the sky had a bright look, as though they were only pretending to be clouds. (Are the clouds that hover over Fife the authentic silver-lined ones?) The countryside had a fresh, well-cared-for look and the well-tilled fields of little farms seemed to stretch right down to the sea, as though the thrifty Fife farmer could only thole to stop at the water's edge. You will not find a prettier sweep on all the coast than Largo Bay. Spring sunshine paints its colours brightly, dimpling blue of the sea, red tiles on an odd farm, soft green of the links dotted with the fleecy white of grazing sheep. The Bass Rock suddenly came into view again through the clear light over the blue water, and it needed a hasty glance at the map to reassure one that it had a perfectly good right to be there. A deeply indented coast-line never seems to lay itself out as tidily as you would expect from the map, and each corner seems as if it were the end of the world, only to open out into an infinity of further corners as soon as you have passed. This bewildering succession of sharp corners is always happening to you in Fife, but Largo Bay has a wide and generous sweep, and you need not always be hunting round the corner.

While, according to the old rhyme, the lasses in Leven were bonnie (which I would not doubt) in Largo they were all "saucy limmers." I do not know how saucy they are to-day. The only lassie

we saw along this road, under the shadow of green
Largo Law, was no saucy limmer, but the demure
and extremely efficient driver of a milk-lorry, and,
in the modern world, it is an everyday thing, and no
sign of sauciness, for a bonnie lassie to bring round
your morning milk by motor.

Largo has had at least two famous sons. One
was Sir Andrew Wood, captain of the gallant *Yellow
Carvel*, which beat off the raiding ships of England,
when James the Fourth was King. A picturesque
and romantic figure was Sir Andrew, as splendidly
handsome as he was brave. It was he who encouraged his king to make Scotland strong at sea, for
those were the days when new visions were opening
to the world of traffics and discoveries, of golden
adventures on the main. In pursuance of this
dream of sea-power, King James built the *Great
Michael*, a mighty man-o'-war of her day. All the
carpenters in the land gave to the building of her
the labour of a year and day. "They cut down all
the forests of Fife for her timbers," says the old
story, "and cumbered all Scotland to get her to sea."

But it was not in this giant that the brave Sir
Andrew won his sea-fight. With his famed *Yellow
Carvel* and a tiny sister-ship, the *Flower*, he beat off
five English raiders that were plundering the shipping in the Forth, and took their captains prisoner.
The English, hitherto undisputed masters of these
waters, smarted under this reverse, and their king
offered high rewards to any sea-captain who would

94

take Sir Andrew prisoner. Stephen Bull, a bluff English sea-dog, set off on this quest with three great ships, swearing to bring back his prisoner, alive or dead. Nearing the Firth of Forth, he took the crews of some fishing-boats captive and sailed on. Two ships appeared on the horizon, and Bull demanded of his prisoners if these were the *Yellow Carvel* and the *Flower*. At first, the canny Fife fishermen told him that they could not say, but when he had promised them their life and liberty whichever way the fight went, they admitted that the ships were Sir Andrew's. The battle began in a spirit of chivalrous sportsmanship which is dear to the heart of the fighting sailor. Each skipper broached a great cask of wine and bade every man drink to his fellows. Then they joined battle, three against two, and throughout the long summer day they pounded each other with their heavy clumsy ordnance. So terrific was the cannonade and so fierce the spirit of the fight, that all sense of seamanship was lost and the ships drifted, spitting fire, along the Fife coast to the mouth of the Tay. But wherever the battle may have ended, it ended in a victory for the brave *Yellow Carvel*, and Stephen Bull, who had sailed in hope of easy triumph, found himself led a prisoner before the Scottish king. The chivalry of the sea prevailed, however, for—rare boon for a prisoner in rough times—he was courteously treated and sent home.

"Tell your king," was the message he took with

him, "that we have as manly seamen in Scotland as ever he has in his own country. Let him send no more captains on such errands, for they will receive an even warmer welcome next time."

Sir Andrew preserved the glorious tradition of the retired sea-dog to the last, for when he left the sea, he scorned, though a good churchman, to walk to the kirk on Sundays, but had a canal cut from his house at Largo to the village church, and along this canal his retainers solemnly rowed him every Sabbath in an eight-oared barge.

Largo's other great man was no high admiral, but a scapegrace sailor, who got into trouble at home, sailed with Dampier and was marooned for four years on the lonely island of Juan de Fernandez, where he was "monarch of all he surveyed." But Alexander Selkirk's adventures, strange and authentic as they were, would never have become immortal but for that prince of journalists, Daniel Defoe. Defoe, being the greatest of journalists, had no concern with truth; instead, he invented a method of narrative which, while it was neither truth nor fiction, was stranger, and more enthralling, than either. Defoe did not meet Selkirk at Largo, though he may well, in his journeyings through Scotland, have passed that way. It was at Wapping, probably in a sailors' tavern, that they met, and from the strange outlandish story that Selkirk told over his ale came the immortal classic that is called *Robinson Crusoe*, the most English book ever written. It has always intrigued me to know what Alexander Selkirk thought of *Robinson Crusoe*. Would any flesh-and-blood adventurer feel kindly disposed towards his fictitious ghost who had become a hundred times more famous than himself? It is hardly possible. I can imagine a lively dialogue between the two, but Selkirk would go back to Largo in disgust and defeat, leaving the fictitious Crusoe as victor, for Crusoe represents the triumph of an all-conquering modern truth: that if you have a good press, the facts do not matter in the least. My sympathies are all with Alexander, and I hope that, when he went back to Largo after his wanderings, he found many friendly listeners for his queer true tales.

Kilconquhar, which the older people (who should know best) call Kinneuchar, lies, with its finely-towered church, near a tiny loch, a little to the north-east of our road. Not far from here is Balcarres, home of the earls of Crawford and Balcarres, the present holder of which title has done so much for the preservation of old and lovely things in the countryside. Here, looking out over Kincraig, Lady Anne Lindsay wrote the sorrowful song of Auld Robin Gray. There really was a Robin Gray, but the sad misfortunes of his young sweetheart were mainly imaginary, and Lady Anne, it is to be feared, wrote of them with her tongue in her pretty cheek. . . . "I have been writing a ballad, my dear; I am oppressing my heroine with many misfortunes. I have already sent her Jamie to sea, and broken her father's arm, and made her mother fall sick and given her Auld Robin Gray for a lover; but I wish to load her with a fifth sorrow in four lines, poor thing! Help me to one, I pray. . . . 'Steal the cow, sister Anne,' said the little Elizabeth. . . ." And that is how the cow came to be stolen. What a delightful sidelight on the way in which pathetic ballads are written! Nor does it matter in the least, for that melody would still tug your heartstrings, however cynical you might feel about the cow.

We drove into Elie by a curving landward road and saw, across the roofs of the little town clustering round, a tall kirk spire, some time before we reached it. There are those who say that Elie has lost its ancient beauties and become a mere "sea-side place," but, for myself, I found it a delectable little spot. We ran down a slipway and round the harbour bar, so that we could turn about and face the town from the seaward side. Still there was colour everywhere, a sharper and brighter colour than one usually associates with cooler climes. Sunlight fell on the irregular lines of grey and white houses along the quay, lighting up the red of tiled roof and spire. Sea-birds swooped by with a flash of white. Several more splashes of colour stood out from scarlet bollards set in grey stone and the red cap of a little lighthouse. The blue of the sea glittered and danced, and a crisp salty breeze gave the air a keen savour to the nostrils. Why should there not be air-tasters, as there are wine-tasters? Surely nostrils and lungs are as capable of being educated as that pampered thing, the palate. Certainly, if there were a Government air-taster, he would be able to speak in terms of true appreciation of this marvellous air on the coast of Fife. Probably he would order special vintages, as found at Elie, to be bottled and sold at a colossal price per dozen, in less invigorating neighbourhoods. "Ah," he would say to his fellow-connoisseurs, "sniff that, my boy. Elie, 1932. There's a vintage for you. There's bouquet. . . ." And if ever a grandmaternal government thinks of founding such a post, I shall be willing, from purely altruistic motives, to apply for it. . . . Here on half-sandy, half-grassy stretches fishing-nets hung in the sun, between rows of poles, and the road by which we drove back from the sea was so quiet and deserted that we had to stop and remove a doll's perambulator which had been left in our fairway. We left Elie with a song singing in our ears; a song of gleaming blue water, of nets drying in the sun, of red-tiled, white-walled cottages nestling together in ever so friendly a fashion. The sea still danced in the blue glitter of the spring morning, and the Bass Rock, persistent old friend, still silently hailed us. "You can't get away from me," said the Bass Rock. On we sped past trim little farms with their bee-hive ricks, while an aeroplane zoomed above us, playing hide-and-seek, it seemed, with the fleecy clouds of intense white. We saw a ruined castle on the cliff just before coming into the next little burgh.

This is Newark—one of the three Newark Castles in Scotland. The Fifeshire Newark was the home of David Leslie, that doughty soldier of fortune and misfortune, who routed Montrose at Philiphaugh, not far from the Selkirk Newark, and was himself overwhelmed by Cromwell at Dunbar. A sturdy straightforward soldier, he was unmoved by victory or misfortune and ended his days at Newark in quiet.

Once, in Newark, a handsome young Lindsay who had come out in the Fifteen and was fleeing for his life, was concealed by a romantic young lady and fed with scraps of food which she carried away from the table with such skilful secrecy that her family feared that she was over-eating in a most unlady-like manner. I hope the story had as happy an ending as it deserved to have.

And now we were coming to St. Monan's, where a special treat awaited us. . . .

VI

DOO-COTS AND SALMON-NETS

I hae laid a herrin' in saut—
Lass, gin ye lo'e me, tell me noo;
I hae brewed a forpit o' maut
And I canna come ilka day to woo.

IF you ask which is the most enchanting of the little
Fife fishing towns I shall pretend to weigh the
matter very judiciously and tell you I have not yet
made up my mind, but if you press me, I shall
probably whisper "St. Monan's," making this
admission without the least disrespect towards Elie,
Anstruther or Crail. A man is entitled to a personal preference, so long as he is not too dogmatic.
I once heard of two Englishmen, wrecked on a
tropical island, who fought seventeen rounds with
fists and coco-nut-shells, because óne of them said
that Burnley was a more beautiful town than Bolton.
While I appreciate their motives and admire their
spirit, I do not believe that such a question is to be
settled by fighting. When a man maintains that
Loch Lomond (or the duckpond at Steeple Bump-
stead) is the finest sheet of water in the world, he is
using what might be called a comparative superlative,
and only means that he likes his own particular loch
(or duckpond) better than yours. So if I say that
St. Monan's is the finest of the Fife fishing-towns, I
am expressing a personal preference, about which I
do not wish to fight you. Another point in St.

Monan's favour is that while my artist friends, who have painted round this coast, have some special favourite spot of their own, they all agree, almost automatically, on giving St. Monan's second place, and that is probably the best evidence you could have.

We drove down by steep winding streets to the harbour and there found as brightly colourful a picture as could be seen in any continental port. The whole scene was lit with glowing colour and even the rocks round the harbour had a luminous tint, as if a giant's jewel-case, containing, among other treasures, a special supply of garnet brooches, had been flung higgledy-piggledy into the water. I should not like to say offhand that any colour was *not* represented on those rocks washed by spray and gleaming in the sunlight. There were at least a dozen boats in the little rocky harbour lying at the foot of a brae up which queer, huddled houses climbed steeply, and their gay colouring was a revelation and a joy. I should like to hear what one of our great theatrical producers, who specialise in spectacular effects, would say, if he were suddenly dumped down on St. Monan's quay. Would he be able to reproduce anything so effective as the reds and white and greens of the fishing-boats? Perhaps he might manage the reds and greens, but I will swear the blue would defeat him. That blue which is the favourite colour of the St. Monan's boat-painter has to compete, on a shining spring day, with the blue of sea and sky, but it holds its own, bravely, standing up clearly and vividly. This painting must be kept up continually, and on most of the boats we saw fishermen, wearing what looked like khaki canvas jumpers, painting away steadily and with apparently solid artistic appreciation of their work. I thought of my artist-friends and their pretty pale little water-colours, and wondered if they got such an artistic "kick" out of their job. I should hardly imagine they did. After all, there must be something more zestfully uplifting in dealing with a large pot of brilliant cobalt or scarlet paint and a herring boat-bow than with a small box of water-colours and a sheet of cartridge-paper. Let smaller artists talk of self-expression! In splashing a herring-boat scarlet there must be something of that joyous abandon which goes to the making of the phrase, "painting the town red." Chesterton could write a wonderful poem about it. It is something large, human and exciting, satisfying what psychologists would call a deep soul-need.

"Now don't," said Balaam, eyeing me disapprovingly, "tell me that when you are old you will come and paint boats at St. Monan's." But when I laughed, he added grudgingly: "I admit these chaps make a better job of it than your high-souled artists would do." And I will swear he was itching to seize hold of paintbrush himself.

We heard a pleasant clink of hammers from a big boat-shed on the edge of the harbour. From the open doors of the shed, the ribs of a boat protruded, looking rather like the skeleton of a whale, and two men in canvas jumpers were hard at work on her. Balaam chatted with a handsome, grizzled old man, whose face looked as if it had been pickled in salt and sunshine.

"I should like a bathe out there," said Balaam, pointing to the gleaming water beyond the coloured rocks.

"Ah, weel," said the fisherman, puckering his brown cheeks into a peculiarly Fifish smile, "I was thinkin' of goin' for a wee drink, so ye'll have tae wait till I've had one, afore I come and pu' ye out."

St. Monan's is delightful, perhaps, because it is so exactly typical of what a great writer has called "the little burghs and sea-villages, with their poor little havens, salt-pans and weather-beaten bits of cyclopean breakwaters."

However poor this little haven may be, it is rich in beauty. . . . The lovely red church completes, and seems to bless, the line of odd irregular tiled roofs as you look back on St. Monan's from the harbour. The grey steeple is neither slender nor graceful, but it fits perfectly into the outline of the picture. St. Monan's is fortunate in having what few Scottish villages have, a really old church which neither Reforming zeal nor fierce tempests have been able to destroy. In this church the village folk worshipped before John Knox's time and they worship there still. The old story tells that David the Second and his queen were saved from shipwreck

UNLOADING HERRINGS, ST. MONANS

"O joyfu's the din, when the boats come in,
    When the boats come in sae early;
When the lift is blue, and the herring-nets fu',
    And the sun glints on a' things rarely."

on this shore and that the king vowed to build a church in gratitude for his deliverance. Not merely was he saved from drowning; he was freed, by a miracle, from a poisoned barb while he prayed at the tomb of St. Monan, who had once lived in a rocky hermitage upon the shore. (Sicknesses were cured by the touching of this saint's bones.) The church has one finely carved canopied tomb, but, to me, its most treasured possession would seem to be the little ship that hangs in one of the transepts. A ship in a church? Why not, since most of the worshippers are men of the sea. Churches are everywhere and so is the Divine Presence without which they were built in vain, but in the old church of a fishing village where the little ship hangs, you cannot walk without a deeper humility, for there straying thoughts are drawn, more strongly than in any grand cathedral, to Him who walked the waves of Galilee and did not scorn to choose His friends from fisherfolk.

Pittenweem, a rich, Fifish-sounding name, means the "town of the Cave." Here can be seen the ruined conventual buildings of what was once a great priory belonging to the Austin Canons, who also had property on the Isle of May, where still stands the ruined chapel of St. Adrian, martyred by Norse pirates. (Now the Isle, to which local folk refer simply as "The May," has a modern light-house, and in early times it had a beacon, which the kindly Laird of Barns, of whose sad daughter I shall tell you presently, kept kindled for the guidance of storm-swept vessels.) St. Adrian was buried in a stone coffin, which, according to the custom of stone coffins when they bore the body of a saint, floated to the mainland, but reached, not Pittenweem Priory, but the sands a little farther north. The Priory he founded was a place of frequent pilgrimage where the sick were healed and whence childless women went home to receive the desire of their hearts. Caves were the favourite resting-places of the early saints, but they also had, in later years, a strong appeal to those decidedly unsaintly characters, the rough old free-traders. It was at Pittenweem that the first strands were woven of the cord that was to hang Captain Porteous from an Edinburgh barber's pole. Wilson and Robertson, two daring smugglers, robbed the Kirkcaldy exciseman at Pittenweem. They were brought to trial in Edinburgh and, as you will read in *The Heart of Midlothian*, a daring and devoted effort on the part of the elder man allowed the younger to escape.

The tale shows the courage and devotion of a Fife smuggler. There were Fife lads, too, in the crowd that brought Porteous to grim justice. It is strange for a little town to have lived in two such traditions—that of the holy monks and of the bold smugglers—but queer things happen in Fife. It has even another tradition, unpleasanter than either of the other two, for it was noted for witches and their burnings, a horrible business. There is an old poem, "The Witch of Pittenweem," and at one time the plague of witches was considered so serious that King James the Sixth, that expert in demonology and witchcraft, was consulted about it.

We came to Anstruther, still running past fields that were tilled to the shore. There are two Anstruthers—Wester and Easter—but they run together, so that there is a much longer sea-front than at St. Monan's. This seemed to me foreign-looking and not as characteristically Fifish as some of the other little burghs, perhaps because the colours were not so concentrated and the houses, with their crow-stepped roofs, not so huddled. At a first glance that cobbled foreshore road might have belonged to some coast town in Belgium or Holland. There were fishing-boats in the harbour, resting, not in blue water, but in oozy mud. Some of the names of the boats gave a mingled flavour of piety and romance, for among those that we saw were Mizpah, Ebenezer and Fisher Lassie.

The most notable incident in Anstruther's history was the drifting and wrecking of some ships of the Spanish Armada on its shores. The old chronicler tells of this happening in splendid language: "The Lord of Armies, Wha ryddes upon the ways of the winds, the Keippar of his own Israel, was in the meantime convoying that monstrous navie about our costes, and directing their hulks and galiantes to the ylands, rokkes and sands, wharupon He had destinat thair wrack and destruction."

Though the Armada had set out with such grandiose and arrogant intentions, the survivors who landed at Anstruther, storm-tossed, famished and half-drowned, considered themselves very fortunate to be kindly treated. Anstruther showed a forgiving hospitality and did not send them hungry away. Up to the time of the Union Anstruther's trade was flourishing, but after that it dwindled, though, however meagre legitimate trade might be, there always seems to have been plenty of smuggling. There were Fife free-traders in the mob that Porteous fired on, and it was an Anstruther youth named Birrel who brought the hempen rope that did the hanging.

But Anstruther can boast of a more illustrious and infinitely more respectable son, Dr. Thomas Chalmers. You will see his lithographed portrait, piously framed, in many an old-fashioned Fife cottage. Chalmers was one of the apostles of an impressive nineteenth-century piety—a religion that linked itself with thrift, austerity and stern endeavour.

They will show you a spot on the sands between Anstruther and Pittenweem, where he would come, as an austere youth, and preach to the waves. Of his impressiveness there was no doubt, nor of his passion for method, for, they said, he would not swing his walking-stick, except by the rules of arithmetic.

Cellardyke is practically joined to Anstruther

Photo by Valentine & Sons, Ltd.

BILLOWNESS, ANSTRUTHER

"Anstruther . . . where ships of the Spanish Armada
drifted and foundered . . ."

Easter. Here the haughty Cardinal Beaton, who was murdered in revenge for the martyrdom of Wishart, used to land, breaking his journey to St. Andrews, and he is said to have been buried in the churchyard of Kilrenny, over the brae beyond, though terrible things happened to his body before it reached a quiet grave. This coast has its share of strange guests—saints, reformers, Covenanting and Jacobite fugitives, smugglers and pirates. Paul Jones, who must often have scanned Fife shores, contemplated a raid but thought better of it.

If any little Fife town is to dispute the pre-eminence of St. Monan's it will be Crail. Here is another little haven with its curving grey sea-wall, and here are clusters of red-tiled houses with crow-stepped gables, clambering up the hill-sides. The town hall is as Dutch-looking as anything in Dysart, and everything about the place has an air of colour, "foreign-ness" and oddity. Its church, with its gaunt steeple, though not so old as St. Monan's, is of a goodly age, and its grey aisles once reverberated with the sound of John Knox's first thunderings against the Scarlet Woman. Here, too, Archbishop Sharpe—he was done to death by Balfour of Burleigh on Magus Moor—ministered before he forswore the Covenanting faith. There is a tombstone in the vestry which tells one of the most sorrowful tales. All death is sad, but what can be more heart-breaking than the death of a bride? The poet Drummond of Hawthornden was betrothed to the beautiful Miss Cunningham, daughter of the Laird of Barns. She died the day before her wedding and she was only nineteen. . . .

Crail has a Blue Stone, which is not so hard to kiss as the Blarney Stone, for it lies at the side of the road near to the church. Crail folk have no right, perhaps, to regard this stone with so much affection, because it is really a missile, flung by the devil at Crail Church. It missed its mark, but it was a splendid throw, because he hurled it from the Isle of May, which is at least seven miles off. When I was a boy, I saw C. B. Fry, fielding like an angel on the boundary at Lord's, but even he never achieved such a mighty throw-in. And if you would doubt the story, Crail will show you his thumb-print—the devil's, I mean, not Mr. Fry's—and, if you are not convinced then, evidence means nothing to you.

Crail is famous for crabs and for capons. A Crail capon is a genuine *rara avis*, for it is no bird at all, but a fish. A haddock smoked in the chimney is the real Crail capon, and a hungry man will find nothing tastier.

There is no motor-road round Fife Ness, but it is very well worth while to make the run and come back again into Crail. We ran along to this rocky point —the extreme corner of a land of corners—under a blue sky, with farm-lands on our left and green links on our right. Here was the edge of things, for we could go no farther eastward. Southern seas could hardly be bluer than was the Firth that after-

Photo by Valentine & Sons, Ltd.

CRAIL

"Little haven . . . grey sea-wall . . . clusters of red-tiled houses."

noon. It shimmered lazily, with no hint of black storms that could lash it in winter-time. A line of warships was strung out, steaming, no doubt, towards Rosyth.

Over the brae is the Castle of Balcomie, where was welcomed, after her landing nearby, Mary of Guise, who came to be the bride of James the Fifth. Their child was the daughter of sorrow, of whom the broken, dying father said: "It came with a lass, and it will go with a lass."

We turned back towards Crail, and then took the northern road towards Kingsbarns. The barns were the corn-barns of the Castle of Falkland, where the Duke of Rothesay was starved to death and where James the Fifth died broken-hearted, after the rout at Solway Moss.

Still the sun shone on sea and land, making a symphony of blue and gold—blue of the water and gold of the gorse "on the knowes where the broom stands braw."

Then suddenly we came round a sweeping curve and saw St. Andrews on its curving bay below us and a dim pearly panorama of coast-line stretching into the haze beyond. We saw the grey city, with its towers and pinnacles, over the roofs of a newly-grown suburb, and once more modernity helped rather than offended, for those red roofs, however "wrong" they might be when you were near them, gave a bright splash of colour that lit up the grey.

All seemed quiet and grave as we drove in by the

Crail road under the shadow of sombre walls, and then we saw an even vivider splash of colour against the grey, as two girl students went laughing by, in gowns of scarlet.

VII

CITY OF THE SCARLET GOWN

> . . . . the little town,
> The drifting surf, the wintry sea,
> The college of the scarlet gown,
> St. Andrews by the Northern Sea,
> That is a haunted town to me.
>
> ANDREW LANG.

SOBER grey with that touch of smiling scarlet—
there you have the colour and the key of St.
Andrews. The town is solemn and hoary, bowed
beneath the burdens of antiquity and learning, yet
the scarlet gown will tell you, and tell you truly,
that bright youth is eternal, and as much a part of
life as age, however wise. As her own youthful
poet sang:

> "Grey in thine age, there yet in thee abides
> The force of youth, to make thyself anew
> A name of honour and a place of power. . . ."

We drove in under the grey Abbey Wall and
passed the western end of St. Leonard's College,
which Dr. Johnson visited, "after supper, the landlord walking before with a candle, and the waiter
with a lantern." The great antiquities of the city
were on our right between the magic arches of the
Pends and the sea, but we turned first to go slowly
along South Street, a wide and gracious thorough-
fare, shaded with lime trees.

There was something of the atmosphere that holds

113

you when you first walk along the Broad at Oxford. Is it a real resemblance, or are you only moved by the age and greyness, by the air of real serenity, mingled with a touch of academic sedateness, which does no harm to anyone, and is almost charming in its proper place? I do not know.

South Street is only one of three parallel main streets, but it impresses you more by its breadth and dignity than the others. If a street is worthy to be named with Princes Street, Edinburgh, here it is, and Princes Street has no green avenue of limes. Here is a street, where you might also spend a holiday, walking slowly back and forwards between the Pends and the West Port. What would you see? You would see the house where Mary Queen of Scots spent some of her few care-free days, and then St. Mary's College, where, in the quadrangle, still grows the thorn-tree that she planted. Opposite, is the Town Church, which, frankly, does not look in the least like the place where John Knox preached his first sermon. No one can tell how many times it has been altered and rebuilt since it was first founded in 1412, but nothing about its exterior now looks very old, except its brave tower, which remains sturdily in the spirit of the rebels—Reformer or Covenanter—who, beneath it, denounced evil in high places.

As you come nearer to the West Port, you will see, in the grounds of Madras College, a beautiful creeper-covered fragment of the Blackfriars Chapel. The Reformers did not destroy so many beautiful places as their enemies have claimed, but the wrecking of this lovely spot must, I fear, be placed to their discredit.

At the grey and solid West Port we turned again, for South Street cannot be traversed too often, and came slowly back to the Pends, those two Gothic archways which open the way to an even older St. Andrews, where the towers of the Cathedral and St. Rule stand up, looking over Fife, Angus and the sea.

The modern mind suffers most from its worst affliction—self-consciousness—when it visits old and holy ground. As we walked under the Pends, we were graceless moderns looking at old and beautiful things. Yet when Johnson and Boswell drove into St. Andrews "after a dreary drive, in a dusky night," just a hundred and fifty years ago, they, too, were moderns, looking at old things. That is why it is difficult to find and keep a true perspective. Johnson's reactions—horrid word—to pure beauty may be judged by his literary criticism, which is an almost perfect touchstone of what *not* to like, and he never went to any place prepared to ecstasise over its beauties. He measured it against the slide-rule of his splendid prejudices and then pushed it away. Well, that is a point of view. It is not mine, because my prejudices are not splendid, and, such as they are, they are always contradicting each other. Burke said of Boswell: "You have so much good nature that it is scarce a virtue." A cap that fits me exactly, for my habit of liking to like things is a vice. Yet there is always something attractive about an honest Philistine, and his prejudices may do stout work, in sweeping aside a mass of sham artistic nonsense. The lovable thing about Johnson, as with all really good Tories, is that your violent disagreement with them does not make you like them any less. His bark was as cheerful as your own favourite dog's, and he seldom really bit anything that did not deserve to be bitten.

It would have been possible, I think, to follow Johnson as he stumped round the Cathedral ruins, without being seriously offended. True, he had to have his fling at John Knox first. When he was asked where Knox was buried, he flung out: "I hope in the highway." (As a matter of fact, Knox *was* buried in what is now a highway, for the old church-yard of St. Giles, Edinburgh, is now Parliament Square.) He would have liked to mount the steeples, but was told that one of them was unsafe. Wickedly he hoped that it might remain in its shaky position: "For," said he, "it may fall on some of the posterity of John Knox, and no great matter." But the most telling point he made against Knox was this: "Differing from a man in doctrine is no reason why you should pull his house about his ears." No prejudice that, but a shining golden rule.

Once the Doctor's prejudices were appeased, he could look on fine things, and understand them. He walked, as we walked, where, rising above quiet graves, the noble eastern gable stands, pinnacled by twin spires. Even if he did not venerate pure beauty as we understand it to-day, he might reasonably argue that to neglect a religion and yet gush over its ruined fanes, showed a feebly canting turn of mind. His great voice boomed through the quiet cloisters, in condemnation of the Reformers who "set on a mob, without knowing where it would end." Under the influence of those cloisters, too, he spoke of the monastic life, not merely with sense, which he had in plenty, but with a rare graciousness. "I never read of a hermit, but in imagination, I kiss his feet; never of a monastery, but I could fall on my knees and kiss the pavement. But I think putting young people there, who know nothing of life, nothing of retirement, is dangerous and wicked."

He who has never been tempted to fall on his knees and kiss a cloistered pavement can have no imaginative sense of the beauty and tranquillity of the old religious life, and nowhere is that feeling stronger than under the shadow of the ruined towers of St. Andrews Cathedral. It took over a hundred and fifty years to build, and Bruce himself, four years after Bannockburn, knelt at its consecration.

John Knox preached four thunderous sermons there against Popish idolatry, but Johnson was wrong in saying that Knox, or the mob that he set on, pulled the Cathedral down. Although

> ". . . wi' John Calvin in their heads
> And hammers i' their hands and spades,
> Enraged at idols, mass and beads,"

they broke many a beautiful statue and ornament, they did not "ding the Cathedral down." Raging east winds and the crueller forces of neglect and decay had made the lovely place a ruin by Cromwell's time and, just as happened at Dundrennan Abbey and other places, the stones were taken away by anyone who wanted them for building. It was a crime of crimes that a beautiful church should be used as a mere stone-quarry, but no one can blame John Knox for that.

It is rather amusing that Johnson, while visiting the Cathedral, should have failed to see the ancient square tower of St. Rule, which is so tall and so near. (It is as if a foreigner were to visit the National Gallery and not notice Nelson's Column.) When angry Scotsmen complained that he had not mentioned it in his book, Boswell took up the cudgels in his defence: "I am afraid the censure must fall on those who did not tell us of it." A delicious excuse, which I hereby hand on to critics of my own shortcomings.

The tower is stout and square enough to be seen miles away, but it preserves, in sphinx-like silence, the secret of its origin. Archæologists still quarrel over the date of its first building, but none would put it later than the early twelfth century. Even if the church of which so little remains was built then, it is likely that the tower itself dated from several centuries earlier, and the legend remains strong that here St. Rule brought the sacred relics of St. Andrew

—three fingers and two toes. Scott, as a lusty young man, climbed the hundred and fifty dark stairs to gaze out over The Antiquary's country, but on his last visit to St. Andrews he felt no wish to climb, but sadly wrote in his Journal:

"I did not go up to St. Rule's Tower as on former occasions; there is a falling off, for when before did I remain, sitting below when there was a steeple to be ascended? But the rheumatism has begun to change that vein for some time past, though I think this is the first decided sign of acquiescence in my lot. I sat down on a grave-stone, and recollected the first visit I made to St. Andrews, now thirty-four years ago. What changes in my feeling and my fortune have since then taken place! some for the better, many for the worse. I remembered the name I then carved in Runic characters on the turf beside the castle-gate, and I asked why it should still agitate my heart. But my friends came down from the town, and the foolish idea was chased away."

What was the name he carved? It was that of an old sweetheart, who, just as he did, happily married someone else. He spoke of himself as "broken-hearted for two years, my heart handsomely pieced again, but the crack will remain to my dying day . . ."

The castle ruins stand on a grim rock, fiercely besieged by the sea. Even for a rock-girt hold, the castle of St. Andrews, with its Sea Tower and Bottle Dungeon, has an air of fierce truculence, if not of cruelty. It bears also a shattered look, as though only the ferocity of the elements could have broken its haughty and arrogant spirit—a spirit inseparably linked with that proud Cardinal who caused the martyrdom of Wishart and was himself slain there by desperate men.

It was a bishop's palace, but few bishops were men of peace in the troubled times of Scotland's history. Little or nothing remains of what Bishop Roger built in 1200. The English and the sea between them destroyed it, and it had to be rebuilt by another bishop two centuries later. James III, as hapless as any of his hapless house, was born there—born to perish under an assassin's dagger, and later the storm of the Reformation raged round it, even more fiercely than the sea at its rocky base.

Its grimmest, most desperate tale is that of Wishart, Beaton and Leslie. The proud Cardinal, who was king of Scotland in all but name, sought to crush the Reformers with an iron and arrogant hand, and flung George Wishart, a man of integrity and simple piety, much loved by the people, into his castle dungeon—a shuddering, evil place to this day. There was a mockery of a trial in the Cathedral, and Wishart, after being hooted down by his accusers, was condemned to be burnt at the stake. The martyrdom was staged opposite the Cardinal's palace, with every circumstance of devilish cruelty. It was to be a piece of deliberate frightfulness, for the smoke of Wishart's burning was to ascend where it might most easily strike terror in the hearts of the people. It was also to be an amusing show, which the Cardinal might watch, lolling on his cushions, from a wall hung with gay tapestries. Wishart was chained to the stake, and, besides the faggots piled at his feet, bags of gunpowder were tied to his body. The martyr gazed up at the lolling Cardinal and then spoke to the captain of the guard:

"May God forgive yonder man," he said, " who lies so proudly on the wall. Soon he shall lie there, not in pomp, but in shame."

So Wishart died, sent, as the old tale says, "by a painful death to a blessed immortality." Within a few days, his grim prophecy was fulfilled. The spark that lit Wishart's pile ignited in the hearts of the people a raging flame of hate against the Cardinal. Norman Leslie, Master of Rothes, swore to rid the land of a callous tyrant, and made his way into the castle at the head of sixteen desperate men. Naturally he could not have taken so strong a castle by open assault, but, early in the morning, he followed the masons who were at work, repairing the fortifications, and, at the head of his ruthless band, slipped in after them. One by one, in grim silence, the Cardinal's servants were seized and flung outside, and a few moments later Leslie was battering at the bolted door of the Cardinal's room, and shouting that, if he did not come out, he would be burnt out, like a rat in a stack. Opening the door, he begged for mercy, but was sternly told that he should receive only such mercy as he had meted to George Wishart. With swords and poniards pointed at his throat, they bade him say his last prayer, and so they stabbed him. Then they dragged his body to the battlements, where, in cushioned ease, he had watched Wishart die, and so the corpse lay, not in pomp or vanity, but in shame. Afterwards the body was "pickled in salt and closit in a kiste," and thrown into the same Sea Tower dungeon where Wishart had been chained.

The murderers now desperately designed to hold the castle and they were joined by many, who, though they did not love murder, rejoiced that a tyrant had fallen. The castle was defended bravely, but at last it fell, and the leaders of the garrison were sent to the galleys. Among these galley-slaves was a dour, bearded man, with smouldering eyes. He was to come to St. Andrews again, and it would have been well for his enemies if they had never chained him to an oar.

I have spoken harshly of those who do not show due reverence in the presence of holy things, and now I am in danger of being hoist with my own petard. Must I confess that I have gazed, dry-eyed, upon the Links of St. Andrews or that I have stood, unmoved, in view of the Royal and Ancient Club-house? I must. Yet why must I hang my head in shame? Who is a little-known and un-distinguished novelist to write of the Golfers' Heaven? I am no impassioned lyrist. I have no

ROYAL AND ANCIENT CLUB HOUSE, ST. ANDREWS

Photo by Valentine & Sons, Ltd.

"Rich and poor alike are smitten with the fever;
    Their business and religion is to play;
And a man is scarcely deemed a true believer,
    Unless he goes at least a round a day."

lute, no lyre, no shawm, no sackbut, no psaltery. How then should I sing of Clubs and the Man?

You have to go right to the opposite side of the town. A local Guide, which I bought at a bookshop for one penny, contains one sentence which alone is cheap at the price. "The hurried tourist," it says, "can obtain a good view of part of the Links, *without leaving the vicinity of the Martyrs' Monument.*" I love that happy touch. No pains are spared, you perceive, to induce a suitably devotional frame of mind.

"There are four courses at St. Andrews," a golfer once told me. "The Old Course is the best course in the world. The Second Course is the second best in the world. The third one is very good indeed, and the fourth is for people like yourself."

The Royal and Ancient Golf Club-house is a big squarish grey building which would appear to consist, on one side at least, almost entirely of bay windows. I would not care to give its architectural handicap in figures, but though it differs in shape, say, from an ancient college or cathedral, it has a solid impressiveness of its own. Here sits the committee of the Royal and Ancient—a sort of Star Chamber or Council of Seven—which rules the golfing world with a club of iron, and here, if anywhere, a man is called on, as the greatest living writer has expressed it, "to see Golf steadily and see it whole."

No doubt this historic building is all it should be,

and yet, perhaps, before I saw it, my wandering fancy had painted a somewhat different picture. The real thing is so very real and, maybe, a trifle pedestrian. Might there not have been a triumphal archway, flanked by Corinthian pillars in the form of giant granite golf-bags surrounded by winged seraphs, clad in plus-fours? Let the Council of Seven place this suggestion on the agenda of their next committee meeting.

Yet, if the peevish sub-golfer may carp, this is indeed Golfers' Heaven, the nearest equivalent to the poet's vision of:

". . . a land of greens and gold, the club-house of the blest,
Where bunkers cease from troubling and the niblick is at rest . . .
Sorrow and slicing are unknown, pulling and pain have passed,
And peace—serene, eternal—fills the golfer's heart at last."

Not that I shall ever reach that fair spot.
"If you can do the Jubilee Course in under a thousand," said Balaam, "I'll eat my hat."
The hat remains uneaten to this day.

*　　　*　　　*　　　*　　　*

But I can forget the badness of my golf, in re-calling what the poet of St. Andrews called the city's "inexplicable grace." He wrote but one tiny volume of verse and he died tragically young, yet he set down the soul of St. Andrews on paper, limning her loveliness as no other poet has ever done:

> "Blue, blue is the sea to-day,
>   Warmly the light
> Sleeps on St. Andrews Bay—
>   Blue, fringed with white." [1]

Truly those whom the gods love die young. They must have loved him very dearly . . .

[1] "A December Day," from *The Scarlet Gown*, by R. F. Murray.

VIII

THE ROAD TO MONTROSE

The lang lift lies abune the world
On ilka windless day;
The ships creep down the ocean line
Sma' on the band of grey.

VIOLET JACOB.

GOLFERS' Heaven was behind us, and we were making for the River Tay, which Scott called the Scottish Tiber. Crossing the Firth of Forth, we had sung "Farewell, Scotland, I'm awa' to Fife!" Soon we should say farewell to Fife and be, according to the old saw, in Scotland again. From St. Andrews, still hugging the breezy coast, we came to the river Eden and the perfect mediæval bridge that spans it. There are Scotsmen who, as we have seen, consider the Forth Bridge a work of Nature, and the Tay Bridge, which we were soon to see, might also reasonably be reckoned one of the world's wonders, and here, between them, was the Guard Bridge, their elder by at least four and a half centuries. You expect the really old Scottish bridge to be tiny, like the single graceful sweep of Tam o' Shanter's Brig o' Doon, but here is something that has length and grandeur. Instead of one arch, it has six, with massively buttressed bays between. I will not pretend it is very broad, for it was built in an age that did not know the wild urge of two charabancs to pass one another, but it fulfils the mediæval ideal of being beautiful and doing its job well. Balaam was disposed to dispute this point.

"No narrow bridge is doing its job well," he objected. "Its job is to get me expeditiously across, and if I have to wait for the other fellow or risk having the paint chewed off my wings, then the bridge is not doing its work efficiently."

"When you get to heaven," I retorted, "you'll still be worrying about someone scraping your wings. Like a good modern, you mistake speed for efficiency. The mediæval philosophy of a bridge was not merely to get you to the other side, but to let you have a good look over as you went. Looking over a bridge was—and should still be— one of the indisputably good things of life. Indeed, I would go so far as to define a gentleman as a man who can look over a bridge with grace and distinction. The good old Bishop who built the bridge knew all about it. That's why he built these jolly little bays."

"The good old days," jeered Balaam. "And an hour ago you were shuddering over the Bottle Dungeon."

"Bottle Dungeons are no more a fair sample of mediæval civilisation than Chicago gangsters are of ours. My point was only that it is better to know where you're going, even if you loiter pleasantly by the way, than to go nowhere at all at ninety miles an hour."

It was difficult not to loiter on the Guard Bridge. If you were to build an ideal mediæval town, you would require certain ingredients: Thaxted church, an Oxford college or two, and some half-timbered houses, say, from Tewkesbury. But you would also need a river and a bridge, and I can offer you nothing better for your purpose than this wonderful Guard Bridge, with its little bays and its six arches. But this ideal old town should remain, you understand, strictly in the imagination. There are very rich Americans who take such an idea literally and somehow actually take our castles home. It would be sinful if such a fate befell the Guard Bridge, and so we must pray that the millionaires may be kept busy playing golf at St. Andrews and not come out to notice how beautiful it is.

Leuchars is chiefly known to the wider world as a railway junction where golfers change for St. Andrews, but it deserves a nobler reputation, if only for its church. Until I saw this church, Leuchars had stuck in my memory as the locus of a Barrie story. A journalist friend of mine was speaker at a dinner at which Barrie was present, and he took as his theme the old-fashioned Scottish passion for education, which led learning-hungry students to seize any kind of work which would help to pay their fees at the University. It was no uncommon thing in those old days for a student to spend his days as a porter at Leuchars Junction, and my friend, in the course of a whimsical speech, gave a vivid, but entirely imaginary, account of his early struggles in that humble capacity. Barrie followed, without batting an eyelid.

"I remember the last speaker well," he said solemnly. "Many's the time I've passed him at Leuchars . . . on my engine."

Nothing remains of Leuchars Castle except a mound, but the church is there for all to see, a standing refutation of the complaint that Scotland is poor in really old and beautiful village churches. It stands high and seems to blend several kinds of architecture. The best part of it is Norman, embellished with strange corbels and gargoyles, but, above its arcaded apse, rises an octagonal lantern-towered belfry which, architects say, would be a fine thing anywhere else, but not there. Still, we must be thankful that so much older beauty survived the Reformation, even at the expense of having a Covenanting belfry-tower tacked to the end of it. Nowhere else, at any rate, will you find so complete a symbol of Scottish religious history.

Now it was to be good-bye to Fife in earnest, for we were making for the Tay ferry by a road where broom glowed golden by the wayside and young beech-trees put forth their tender, trembling green, with a beauty we had not seen since we drove to Inveraray last year.

Newport is literally a new port, for the old historic ferries crossed from Tayport farther east, over a narrower stretch of water. It is of the

perils of the sea outside the Firth that a fine poet
has written his ballad, "The Lichts o' Tay":

"Forgi'e a lassie's hasty words!—The Lord Himsel' can save,
  An' gin He's ta'en my lad frae me then I maun thole the lave;
  But when the haar blaws in frae sea, at endin' o' the day,
  Wae's me, the saut tear blin's my e'e—ye sleepless Lichts o' Tay." [1]

The new town is trim and sedate, its terraced
villas rising in lines from the water. To drive
down the slipway and park the car on the deck of
the clean and roomy ferry-boat is easily done, and,
as the boat is so broad and steady there is nothing
adventurous in it. To cross a wide and shining
Firth, with a greengrocer's van parked on one side
of you and a milk-float on the other, tends to take
the edge off the excitement. The sights that come
to you as something fresh and startling are all part
of someone else's (possibly dull) daily round.

Bells clanged, and the ferry-boat moved off so
gently and steadily that it seemed as if it was the
quay that was sliding away, and we were left to gaze
across an infinitely wider Tay than we had looked
on from the North Inch at Perth, just a year before.

Naturally, the great Tay Bridge grips your
attention. It does not hit you quite as hard at
first, for it has no colossal sweeping arches, which
make the Forth Bridge such a wonder to the eye,
but it has a brave look, braver when you know that
it was a victory, not only over tide and distance,

[1] "The Lichts o' Tay," by Tinsley Pratt.

130

but over one of modern history's most dreadful disasters. On a wild Sunday night of the Christmas week of 1879, the centre spans of the old Tay Bridge were hurled into the water by one of the most terrific storms that ever struck the coast. A northbound train made its way through the darkness of night and storm and simply fell into black nothingness. Not a soul among the eighty-odd passengers was saved. You will find in A. J. Cronin's *Hatter's Castle* a passage—short, but of almost terrifying power—describing the disaster. But human effort was undaunted, and within four years, a new bridge was begun, stronger but less rigid, and slightly curved throughout its length, the better to bear the assaults of the elements. It took five years to build, but it has weathered all storms and ill-omens, and still flings its arm of graceful and sinuous strength across to the Angus shore. In construction it is as much stronger than the old bridge as steel is stronger than iron.

While I looked out across the gleaming water, Balaam, who likes machinery better than "prospects," had gone to look at the boat's engines. Like Wells's Bert Smallways, he does not feel that the world is going round if there is not a rich oily smell and large wheels are not going round, too. I found him earnestly talking to the engineer, who, curiously enough, was not oily in the approved Smallways fashion and did not even seem to feel it his duty to be so.

The engineer was one of few genuine Scotsmen I have met who was not truculently patriotic about it; stranger still, he was one of few engineers I have met who did not think engines, and his own engines in particular, more important than the whole of the rest of the world.

"I was born in Dundee," he said, "and I'll die in Dundee. I won't say I wouldn't die for Dundee, if I got my dander up, but I'd be telling a lie if I let you think that every morning o' the year's as grand as this one. Whiles in winter, there's a wind comes up the Firth that, oh, just jabs ye like a dagger, and I'd be deceiving ye if I told ye it didn't. But," he added quickly, "it's a grand morning, this morning."

He was a travelled man, and had not spent the whole of his life going backwards and forwards on the Firth of Tay. He had spent some years down in Devonshire, and he spoke rather wistfully of a little inn where you could get watercress teas on Sundays, or sit outside on a sunny bench, drinking cider. He showed us some fresh green-stuff, which he was carefully taking home in a string-bag.

"*Creeses*," he said, "and I'll confess there's nothing I like better to my tea, though ma missus is no just partial to them hersel'. I got the habit down in Devonshire, but the folk up here mostly think they're just rabbits' meat. . . ." He grew broadly philosophical. "There's something daftlike about human nature. When I was in Devonshire, walking along green lanes and drinkin' cider—a grand drink for a warm country—ye'd think I'd have been contentit, but was I? *Was I?* I was just wishing maself back in Dundee on a dirty Saturday night. But now, when the east wind comes, skirlin' and slashin' up the Firth, I keep thinkin' o' that wee pub and the cider. Just daft. . . . That's what we all are. Not that I'd say a word against Dundee. You just go and take a look at her from the water, and you'll say she's no' so bad."

We went out forward and took a look at her from the water. Now Dundee may have her detractors. When the adjective "bonnie" is applied to Dundee, I am well aware that reference is being made, not to the third city of Scotland, but to a historical character whom I was brought up not to admire. I have been told of a ballad that contains the lines:

> "O whar got ye that havers-meal bannock,
>   My bonnie young lassie, now tell it to me?
>   I got it frae a sodger laddie,
>   Between Saint Johnstone and bonnie Dundee."

But the city has not usually been considered bonnie. It is not easy to find a big industrial town beautiful, and it is the custom of the æsthetically inclined to murmur "Jute" and pass by on the other side. But. . . .

We did not, you see, gain our first impression

133

of Dundee on "a dirty Saturday night." We saw
the ancient Royal Burgh over an enchanting distance of blue water under a magical spring sky. I
do not know how often you can see Dundee like
that, but I should like to hope that the sight is not
rare. At that moment, in the extraordinary clearness of the air, Dundee looked like one of those
sunny Italian cities that mount in bright terraces
from a Southern river-bank. Something in the
purity of the air seemed to have washed the whole
place clean, and even the smoke of the chimneys
was lost against so great an expanse of clear sky.
Every outline was clean and sharp-edged, a rare
sight in a land which is so often abused for lack of
sunshine. Dundee was certainly looking its best
and we firmly decided, in spite of Balaam's wistful
desire to enquire into the great marmalade question,
that it would be better to do nothing that might
cloud that first bright vision of Dundee, seen from
the Firth.

Modern Dundee has swept away most of its old
monasteries and little remains of what is genuinely
old. Wallace wight, Wishart the Martyr, Hertford, Montrose, Monk and the Old Pretender all
played their part in Dundee's stirring history, but
few material traces of their deeds—good or evil—
are left.

So, as soon as we drove off the ferry-boat, we
assiduously kept to our strict coastal route, preserv-
ing our magic vision of Dundee as an Italian city,

intact. And there, in the mind, that picture will always remain.

We drove past docks and shipping, which at first threatened to be endless, but at last the shipping thinned and we drove through the cheerful seaside suburbs of Broughty Ferry and Monifieth. The name, Broughty Ferry, always reminds me of some irrelevant lines of R. F. Murray, the young poet of St. Andrews:

> "And for his part he thought more highly
>   Of Ellen Terry;
> Although he knew a girl named Riley
>   At Broughty Ferry,
> Who might be, if she only chose
>   As great a star.
> She had a part in a tableaux
>   At the bazaar."

Broughty Ferry, I am told, first grew from the big houses of the wealthy folk of Dundee who wished to get farther out from the city, but as you pass along it by the coast road it displays no air of conscious "nabobbery," but seems only a trim and friendly suburb on the modern "dormitory" plan. It is a modern fashion, and a good one, for those who can, to live away from the city where the work must be done, for who would wish, in the vulgar phrase, "to sleep over the shop," when the country and, in this case, the seaside, are near at hand? We may curse the evil of rushing and transport and heavy traffic, but these things do give a chance of a country or semi-country life to those who, otherwise, would be shut in the city all their days and nights. Carnoustie, which is a little farther along, is an outer suburb of Dundee and a seaside resort for all and sundry as well. I don't know that you will find better sands anywhere along the coast; certainly you will never see them looking more bright and golden than we saw them this day. Not alone can Fife boast of golden fringe. There are strands of gold here, too, with clumps of golden broom on low banks by the wayside as the road shakes itself free from streets and houses.

And now that we were clear of Dundee and its farther seaside playgrounds, we were spinning along the real coast of Angus, with glowing colour—azure of sea and gold of broom—beside us. What did we know of Angus, unvisited? Very little, and that vaguely: firstly, that Angus is the new official name for Forfarshire, though the name itself is surely by no means new. We knew that somewhere, though much farther inland, was the enchanted Barrie country, of weavers and Little Ministers and Windows in Thrums. We knew that Angus was the land of the woman poet who wrote "Tam o' the Kirk," a song that Burns himself might have sung, thinking of his Jean instead of Daddy Auld's discourses. The same poet sang of a country,

Whaur the bonnie Sidlaws stand
Wi' their feet on the dark'nin' land
And their heids i' the licht. . . .

and of the exile in the weariful South, who talks
with the Northland wind and is blinded by the tears
that well up from an aching longing for home.

"But saw ye naething, leein' Wind, afore ye cam' to Fife?
There's muckle lyin' 'yont the Tay that's mair to me than life."
"My man, I swept the Angus braes ye hae na trod for years."
"O Wind, forgi'e a hameless loon that canna see for tears!" [1]

We knew—and this was the last scrap of our
meagre knowledge—that a little farther along the
coast was the town of Arbroath, which had an O,
though we did not know what that O meant, and we
were acquainted with Southey's cheerful tale of Ralph
the Rover and the warning bell, set on the Inchcape
Rock by the good Abbot of Aberbrothock.

"I remember the poem well," said Balaam, "because it was taught me by my governess. You
remember when Ralph the Rover bumped into the
place where the bell ought to have been and tore
his hair? Well, she wouldn't let us say: 'My God,
it is the Inchcape Rock!' We had to say: '*Oh
dear*, it is the Inchcape Rock!'"

We found Arbroath a little red town with a wide
quay, much busier, no doubt, that when Scott, in
The Antiquary, called it Fairport, but not very
bustling, for all that. Arbroath manufactures sail-
cloth, but in an age when even steam is not the latest
thing, I do not see how sailcloth-making can be a
growing industry. We turned in from the harbour
and made our way up the long High Street, to find

[1] "The Wild Geese," from *Songs of Angus*, by Violet Jacob.

the ruins of the old Abbey, and incidentally to
solve what for us had been the problem of the
O of Arbroath. Grey is the prevailing colour of
ruined abbeys in Scotland as in England, but
Arbroath Abbey, following the colour of the town,
is as red as sandstone can be. (I do not, offhand, remember any other red abbey except Devor-
guilla's lovely Sweetheart, near Dumfries.) Johnson
spoke truly when he said that his journey would
have been worth while if he had seen Aberbrothock
and nothing else. The remains show that the
Abbey Church must have been a big one. There
is no north wall, but the south wall of the nave still
stands, and high on the gable of the south transept
is a great round window. This is the celebrated
Round O of Arbroath, which had so mystified us.
The good monks, even before Ralph the Rover's
time, had always a kindly thought for storm-tossed
sailors, and in this Round O window, which could
be seen far out at sea, they kept a light continually
burning. But for this wall and gable and one
great gatehouse tower, there is not much left of this
red abbey which William the Lion founded in
memory of St. Thomas of Canterbury. Fires
seem to have been its bane, for it was twice burnt
while it was a-building, and then again in the twelve-
and-thirteen-hundreds. (I hope these fires were
not caused by the beneficent beacon in the O
window.) If blame, however, must be cast, it
must fall, not on Reforming iconoclasts, but on

those who, through years of neglect, allowed a grand church to fall into decay, and even more on those who stole the stone to build their own houses.

We lunched, following our polite custom, off the special food of the country, which at Arbroath is a smoked haddock. It would be just as invidious to set an Arbroath smokie against a Crail capon as to compare either with the delectable grilled herring, straight from Loch Fyne, which we ate at Inveraray last year; but in these things a man should have a catholic taste. If he will realise that the world is wide, and take good things where he finds them, then he will get more from out of life than the man from Bradford, who grumbled because there is no Yorkshire pudding at the North Pole.

We swung back seaward, after the Abbey and our smokies, and found the coast north of Arbroath as red as red Devon by the sea. We left the road to look for Auchmithie, for that is the place where Scott set his "Mussel Crag" scene of the simple joys and elemental sorrows of the fisher-folk.

Those who know their *Antiquary* will remember that at Mussel Crag was enacted one of the most thrilling rescues in fiction, when Sir Arthur Wardour and his beautiful daughter, Isabella, were caught by the tide, and discovered by Edie Ochiltree, the gaberlunzie man. The reply of the aged beggar when Sir Arthur offered him gold if he could think of a method of rescue has been cited as a proof that Scott was a true democrat in spite of himself.

"Good man," said Sir Arthur, "can you think of nothing?—of no help? I'll make you rich—I'll give you a farm—I'll——" "Our riches will be soon equal," said the beggar, looking out upon the strife of waters, "they are sae already; for I hae nae land, and you would give your fair bounds and barony for a square yard of rock that would be dry for twal hours."

The three were eventually rescued from their perilous rocky ledge in wildly exciting fashion, and those who consider Scott dull (without having read him) are recommended to seize and devour a passage full of thrills. Critics have been amused by the fact that in this passage Scott makes the sun set in the eastern sea, but after all, Scott was a Wizard, and surely a Wizard may be allowed a little licence of that kind.

The road leaves the coast for some miles, coming nearer to it at the red village of Inverkeillor. Here we stopped to watch farm-servants planting their potatoes in the reddest soil I have ever seen. In another field, beyond broomy hedges, we saw a ploughman driving his arrow-straight furrow over the downward curve of the land, as though he would follow his plough into the sea.

A little farther along, the Lunan River runs into beautiful Lunan Bay. Here is, I think, the finest stretch of sand we had seen yet.

The railway crosses the South Esk by a long and handsome viaduct, while the road is content with something less spectacular. This is near Ferryden, of which the Angus poet wrote:

> The brigs ride out past Ferryden,
> Ahent the girnin' tugs,
> And the lasses wave to the Baltic men
> Wi' the gowd rings i' their lugs.[1]

The first you see of Montrose is the slender spire of the parish kirk, and you come into the town by a fine-looking bridge which has the dazzle of Aberdeen granite. On the left is the famous Montrose basin, which, I am told, has a Southend-like quality at low tide, but, as we passed it while the water was in, I will speak no evil of it. Besides being, in the judgment of many whose opinion is to be trusted, the greatest living Scottish poet, Violet Jacob has written three fine prose works, one of which, the splendid Jacobite novel, *Flemington*, has its setting around the Montrose Basin. Montrose has a very fine main street, much wider than you will usually see in Scotland, and from one end of it a statue of Sir Robert Peel looks inscrutably down upon a world that has flung away his principles, and is none the better for it.

Montrose is as old as those ports of Fife that traded with the early Saxons and Danes. Where the Infirmary now stands was a fort, built by Erskine of Dun, in Queen Mary's day. From Montrose, they say, set sail the brave Douglas on his

[1] "The Doo'cot up the Braes," from *Songs of Angus*, by Violet Jacob.

quest to carry the heart of Bruce to the Holy Land, and from here, too, sailed the Old Pretender when the last hopes of the Fifteen had flickered out.

We saw the Town Hall, where Boswell said there was "good dancing-room and other rooms for tea-drinking," but we failed to find the "sorry inn" where the waiter put a lump of sugar into the Doctor's lemonade with his fingers and was called a rascal for his pains! "It put me in great glee," says Bozzy, "that our landlord was an Englishman. I rallied the Doctor upon this, and he grew quiet."

At one time, for reasons which I cannot explain, Montrose seems to have had a large population of queer, canny old ladies, concerning whom many tales are told. The tale I like best is that of the spinster who was asked to subscribe to funds for the forming of a Volunteer company. "Na, na," she said, "I'll no' give a shillin' to get men for King George, when I canna get yin for masel!"

Montrose, called the town of "Gable-Endies," because numbers of its house-ends face the streets, has many shady, spacious avenues, many lovely gardens and three fine golf-courses. Besides its splendidly dry climate—the sunshine statistics are astonishing—it claims to have the finest stretch of clean, firm sand in Britain. An extravagant claim? Not at all. The burgh's motto is: *Mare ditat, rosa decorat* (The sea enriches, the rose adorns. . . .). I do not know where you will find a town more nobly enriched or more charmingly adorned.

IX

A KEEK AT THRUMS

Ye may speak o' heavenly mansions, ye may say it winna grieve ye,
When ye quit a world sae bonnie—but I canna just be sure,
For I'll hae tae wait, I'm thinkin', or I see if I believe ye,
Till ma first braid blink o' heaven an' ma last o' Kirriemuir.

VIOLET JACOB.

"Tell me," said Balaam, "what *are* Thrums?"
"Thrums are the short end-threads of the warp."

"Thank you very much. Now I'm ever so much wiser. But is that a reason for this violent divergence from a route that was to hug the whole coast and nothing but the coast?"

"Ample reason. It would be a very sad thing to be in Angus without taking a peep at Kirriemuir, and as we want to enter Kirriemuir from the south, we had better go to Forfar, where the Barrie family lived for some time, and while we are at Forfar we might well try to see Glamis, and then, if we make a round trip of it we cannot very well help passing through Brechin on the way back. But Kirriemuir is the place."

This explains how we found ourselves travelling across pleasant agricultural country to Forfar, which Barrie, in *The Little Minister*, calls Tilliedrum. A little way out of the town we passed the ruins of Restenneth Priory, which was built on the site of a much earlier church founded by St. Boniface, though, as this good saint was born in Devonshire and spent most of his life in Germany, I do not know what he can have been doing in the neighbourhood of Forfar. The priory, built seven hundred years later, was peopled by monks from Dryburgh, and must have been one of the very few Premonstratensian houses in Scotland. We entered Forfar —a bustling little town which, besides marketing the produce of a wide farming district, has linen and jute mills—by the east end of the High Street and stopped at the Town Hall. We are not usually keen connoisseurs of Town Halls, but Balaam had heard that a famous "Scold's Bridle" was kept there and he was anxious to see it, for he affects misogyny among his other pleasant views.

"It was a short-sighted humanitarianism," he has always argued, "which deprived us of such amenities as the scold's bridle and the ducking-stool. No doubt contemporary conservatives said —and said rightly—that it was the thin end of the wedge. . . . And now the whole world is ruled by women."

When, however, he was told that the famous Forfar bridle was used, not so much for scolding wives as for witches, he lost a good deal of his interest, for even Balaam agrees with me that most of the witches, who were tortured and burned, were poor harmless blethering old bodies, who did harm to no one but themselves. Most of those who confessed to dealing with the powers of darkness

made their confession under torture or the fear of
it. The others must obviously have been wrong
in their poor silly old heads.

The Loch of Forfar lies on the right of the Glamis
road as you go westward out of the town. Somewhere on its banks were fought the last battles
between the Picts and the Scots, and the desperate
men who had murdered Malcolm the Second at
Glamis were drowned in its waters while trying to
cross its ice, which broke under their weight.

Balaam was impressed by Glamis Castle, in spite
of himself. He had been prepared to be sceptical
about it.

"You remember last year," he said. "The
neighbourhood of Inverness simply *bristles* with
castles where Macbeth murdered King Duncan,
and now, in an absolutely different part of Scotland,
here is another of them. I can only think that
Macbeth, after the success of the first performance,
took the murder on tour."

"Nonsense. Macbeth became Thane of Glamis,
according to the witches' prophecy, through the
death of Sinel, and a king was certainly murdered
at Glamis—there are monuments in the park, sup-
posed to mark the spot—but that was Malcolm the
Second, Duncan's predecessor, and the deed was
done, not by Macbeth, but by the persons unknown
who afterwards perished in the icy waters of Forfar
Loch. I admit that Shakespeare took Glamis
Castle and placed it several miles away on the top

of Dunsinane Hill, but that was reasonable dramatic licence and, in any case, I don't think he ever called it Glamis."

"I don't suppose he would have known how to pronounce it," said Balaam.

Glamis Castle, though wonderfully impressive in bulk and setting, does not, perhaps, look quite so old as its ancient and stormy history can claim, for seventeenth-century additions of turrets are blended with the older, more massive walls. But its whole aspect is one of dignity and majesty and the woods of pine and fir, with which it seems, from the distance, to be shrouded, lend it an air of mystery as deep as of any dark keep to which, in old tales, a mysterious horseman rode at twilight. Most of the stories connected with Glamis are sad or grim. There was a sixteenth-century lady of Glamis who was accused of having sought to encompass the king's death by witchcraft and was burned at the stake, only to be declared innocent long years afterwards.

Everyone, too, has heard of the mysterious haunted chamber whose secret doorway may only be revealed to the heir of the Strathmores and to one other person whom the earl and his son may implicitly trust.

If the tradition of Glamis has been somewhat mysterious and gloomy, at least it may be said that at the present day that tradition holds no sway, for in the minds of a nation Glamis stands not as a

grim mediæval keep but as the home of that enchanting princess of a modern fairy-tale, whom a loyal
and affectionate people call The Little Duchess.
Grim old ghosts there may have been, but a fairy
charm—a sweeter, surer enchantment—has laid
them for ever. . . .

The road that leads to Kirriemuir from Glamis
runs into the road that comes from Forfar not far
from the brae—the most lovable brae in a land of
braes, for there stands the cottage of *The Window
in Thrums*. Well-intentioned hands have tried to
make the cottage a little more presentable, but still
it is only beautiful by association. If you are
looking for a romantic diamond-paned lattice, set
in trailing rambler roses, you will be disappointed,
but if your face should fall, that will be your
own fault. It will be because you do not know
that the heart of true romance can lie in a
bare whitewashed but-and-ben, especially if it be
touched by the magic of one who could make
John Darling's top hat a fairy chimney. You
would find a dozen more beautiful cottages in any
English village. It even has a slate roof, instead of
the thatch over which ropes were once flung in the
old days to keep it on. The little window in the
white-washed cot is a window not so much in,
as on, Thrums, for it looks out across the little
valley towards "the auld reid hooses croodit" of
Kirriemuir on the hill. It is a window, not in a
bare cottage, but in something as enchanted, as

brimming with laughter and tears as the little chamber in Cinderella's head. Nor is the house on the brae, where, through her window, Jess watched the pageant of the old brave life in Thrums, the only magic landmark at the head of the brae, for nearby is the douce house called Strathview, where the Barrie family returned from Forfar, and where the sweet mother died, who was all Barrie's heroines in one. Kirriemuir has its own history and its own worth, but there could never have been a magic Thrums but for the tales Margaret Ogilvie told an imaginative boy. Even then the old Thrums, which had a weaver's loom in every other house, had gone. "Before I reached my tenth year," he says, "a giant entered my native place in the night, and we woke to find him in possession. . . . Where had been formerly but the click of the shuttle was soon the roar of 'power,' handlooms were pushed into the corner as a room is cleared for a dance; every morning at half-past five, with a yell, and from a chimney-stack that rose high into our caller air, the conqueror waved for evermore his flag of smoke."

The old Thrums of the handlooms and the weavers in their knee-breeches had gone, but its courage, its devotion, its mingled laughter and sorrow, lived in the tales a mother told for a son of genius to set down with magic pen.

Over the way is the solid farm, which Barrie called T'nowhead, whose honest tenant laughed at

Photo by Valentine & Sons, Ltd.

A Window in Thrums

" A window, not in a bare cottage, but in something enchanted
. . . brimming with laughter and tears.''

the ghost at Muckle Friday Fair, not because he saw it (for he sat at the end of the form where he could see nothing) but "because he had paid his money at the hole in the door like the rest of us." It was at T'nowhead, too, that Sanders Elshioner, the coal-man, and Sam'l Dickie, the weaver, paid their queer court to Bell.

These three historic houses are not in Thrums proper. To come to the centre of the town you must descend the twisting brae-road and climb to the opposite bank towards the red houses which cluster round the square, the meeting-place of steep wynds and narrow closes still. In the square, the great fair, or "Muckley," used to be held on Muckle Friday, a time of delirious joy for the bairns of Thrums, when Corp Shiach would buy "Teuch and Tasty" toffee, which pulled out your teeth but was well worth the money. "The heart of Thrums is a box," we are told in *The Little Minister*, "in which the stranger finds himself suddenly, wondering at first how he is to get out, and presently how he got in." The town-house is round and sturdy and its clock-tower fronts the square. You will not see the outside stair up which The Little Minister rushed, on that wild night of riot when the square was full of weavers armed with pikes and when word was brought by Babbie, the Egyptian woman, that the soldiers who had come to apprehend them had halted at the top of the brae near T'nowhead; a night of angry passions when the minister bade his folk go to their homes in peace, and the taunting, wicked-eyed Babbie told them in scorn not to heed the little man; a night when, worst of all, at her wicked instigation and against his will, he flung a clod of earth and hit the captain of the soldiers on the head. There are many pictures in the book, of the adorable Babbie, "daughter of a summer night, born where all the birds are free," but none more brave than the sight of her dark eyes flashing, calling on the Thrums folk to fight for their liberty.

Bank Street turns up steeply and narrowly to the right of the square, but there you will find a new Auld Licht Kirk instead of the old one. The old gable has been incorporated into the new building, which is red and rather ornate, but . . . it is not the same thing. I have a photograph of the old Auld Licht Kirk—the original Original Secession church—which Sentimental Tommy—who spent his earliest days in London—swore was bigger and lovelier than St. Paul's. The picture shows a bare whitewashed building without porch or spire, with six bleak windows and a biggish door on which notices were posted: the plainest of plain buildings, yet a home of faith and devotion; the place, too, where The Little Minister preached his biting sermons against the wiles of women, and tore from the great pulpit Bible the sacred page on which Babbie had scribbled words that were not sacred at all. You will not find the house at whose window queer cranky Doctor McQueen would sit smoking, nor the "hanky-school," which had a lovely garden in which, on Dr. McQueen's advice, the school-mistress-sisters put up a notice: "Persons who come to steal the fruit are requested not to walk on the flower-beds." The school was kept by Miss Ailie and Miss Kitty and then, after Miss Kitty died, by Miss Ailie alone. It was called the hanky-school, because all the pupils had to bring hand-kerchiefs on which they knelt, during prayers, for the protection of Miss Ailie's carpet. In Quality Street, just as in *Sentimental Tommy*, there was a school kept by two sweet sisters. ("Algebra! It —it is not a very ladylike study, Isabella.") It was in another country. It was in a different age. But I think it was the same hanky-school. . . .

The old white house, that once was the Auld Licht Manse, still looks down towards the back of the Tenements, though now there are houses between. That was why in the old Thrums, the backs of the Tenements were better behaved than the fronts, for the Manse had its eye on them. It was to the Manse that The Little Minister came with his mother when he was twenty-one—she would not take off her bonnet till she had opened all the presses—and it was in the faded parlour that the old minister, "with the beautiful face that God gives to all who love Him and follow His command-ments," said to the young one: "God Himself, I think, is very willing to give one-and-twenty a second chance." It was in the garden that Gavin, in boyish exuberance, jumped over a gooseberry-bush and observed, whilst in the air, three scandalised Auld Lichts watching him from behind a dyke. It was in the garden, too, that Babbie hid from the soldiers on the night of the riot.

In the Tenements of fiction lived Jamie Don, who never married because he thought that the women proposed; Sanders Gilruth, who boasted that "by having a seat in two churches he could lie in bed on the Sabbath and get the credit of being at one or other"; and many another canty character. In a small house in the Tenements of fact, James Matthew Barrie was born. "On the day I was born," he says in the opening sentence of *Margaret Ogilvie*, "we bought six hair-bottomed chairs. . . ." Those chairs are a symbol of the romance that lies at the heart of the old life in a Scots countryside; they speak of passionate family devotion, of the happy fireside clime to weans and wife. When you see the little house in the Tenements, where Barrie was born, your mind goes instinctively to the Burns' cottage at Alloway, for it tells the same story: a devoted, God-fearing father, a beautiful mother, a big family fighting bravely against early poverty, a son of genius. . . . More truly than all the mansions of the great cities, more truly even than the grandeurs of mountain and loch, such a little house is the real Scotland; the Scotland of family love, of weans and wife. Behind the little house is the most romantic wash-house in the world, which (as we have been told in the dedication to the plays) was the first theatre where a Barrie play was performed. He was seven years old and wore a glengarry bonnet. This wash-house—the family wash is still done there on Mondays—was the original of "the house they built for Wendy," though it had no top-hat for a chimney. ("If Robb had owned a lum hat I have no doubt that it would have been placed on the washing-house.") That is the Barrie secret, to bring fairyland from a wash-house, with or without the aid of a lum hat.

There was one more landmark of Thrums that I wanted to see, and that was the Cuttle Well in the Den, not entirely for the sake of Sentimental Tommy, but for the sake of an old school friend—he never came back from the War—who, twenty years ago, copied out these lines into my album: "*First love is but a boy and girl playing at the Cuttle Well with a bird's egg. They blow it on one summer evening in the long grass, and on the next it is borne away on a coarse laugh, or it breaks beneath the burden of a tear. And yet . . .*"

We knew our Barrie, word by word and line by line, in those days, believing, naturally, that we were the only fellows in the world who had read the man. We would put each other through long Barrie examinations, posing such searching questions as: "Who was it lived in the Tenements and kept ferrets?" Or: "What was the favourite poem of Margaret Ogilvie's father?" We *ate*

Sentimental Tommy, and when we read *Tommy and Grizel* we were appalled at Tommy's dreadful end. Together we sat down and wrote a letter to Barrie, demanding that Tommy should be given one more chance. It was a solemnly argumentative letter, not in the least sentimental, and it indicated several ways of bringing Tommy back to life again. The letter was never posted, for at the last moment, my friend, an honester boy than I, recanted, saying that it served Tommy jolly well right. Which was true enough, though I denied it passionately those twenty years ago. . . .

To reach the Den it is best to go back to the Square and start again, working out by your left instead of by your right. It is "round the corner from Thrums," a little glen that is not as wildly romantic as it was when Sentimental Tommy was a boy. (Like all sentimental spots, it was probably not so romantic even then, for Tommy had to pretend to his sister that it was much more marvellous than it really was.) It is like a miniature Pittencrieff; there are trees and wooded slopes, but part of it has been tamed, "and the brae is not shabby." Here was the scene of The Last Jacobite Rising and of the exploits of Stroke and his gallant companions. The Cuttle Well is by no means the "narsty puddle" that Tommy's sister suspected it to be, though it is not what we would call a well.

In the Den, I thought not so much of Tommy and Corp as of two other boys who adored them, but

154

had never been to Thrums; two raw, lanky lads, striding along country roads much farther south, arguing fiercely and chopping off wayside thistles with their ash-plants and stopping every now and then to demand: "What was the name of the Thrums mole-catcher who was sent to prison for boasting?" In those days Tommy and Corp were the Barrie people for our money. We had no time for the womenfolk, but now I have changed my mind, and I am certain my friend would have changed his mind, too, for more living than all the Thrums men-folk are Babbie, whose eyes were "black, black, black, black," and Grizel of the rocking arms and the twisted smile; more living and more beautiful than even these is the mother with the soft face, for they were only dream-women, but Margaret Ogilvie lived, and lives for ever more.

When you have reached the top of the hill above Kirriemuir, you can look down over "the steadin' and the fields" of Strathmore towards where the bonnie Sidlaws stand. A breath-taking view in its very richness of green fields, and darker woodlands with the bonnie hills beyond.

"For it's fules wad bide in London when they kent o'
    Kirriemuir."

Brechin, though it may happen to lie on your road on the way back from a digression, is not to be treated lightly on that account. It is a place well worth seeing for its own sake. The city—you

must remember it is a city, and not a town—is very
old, and its most outstanding landmark is the great
Round Tower, which seems to grow out of a corner
of the Cathedral almost like a giant chimney-stack.
(Or, perhaps, with its cone-shaped turret at the top,
it has more the shape of a gigantic stickless rocket.)
There are many such towers in Ireland but only
one other in Scotland—that at Abernethy. (Whatever archæologists may say of St. Rule's at St.
Andrews, it is not a *round* tower.) No one knows
how old the tower is, but it must be older than the
Cathedral. Some say that the tower is a relic of
Pictish civilisation—Abernethy was the old Pictish
capital and Brechin may have been a Pictish city
—and that it was used as a mausoleum for ancient
kings. Others hold that it was a Danish watch-
tower. But it does not resemble in any way the
other Pictish or Danish relics which are to be found
in the north and west. The strongest evidence
seems to show that it was a part of monastic building, used for penitential retirement. Perhaps it
was there when Brechin was swept with fire and
sword by the Danes nearly a thousand years ago;
if so, it must have looked down upon the winged
helmets of the fierce Norsemen, just as it looked
down later on the mail-shirts of the First Edward's
men-at-arms, and, later still, upon the plumes of
the Cavaliers when Montrose stormed Brechin for
the king. The Cathedral, which was founded by
David the First, happily does not lie in ruins, though

much of the earliest structure has been either replaced or covered up. The Round Tower, along
with the square tower and other spires, gives
the Cathedral a picturesque, but somewhat lumpy,
appearance. Brechin Castle is nearby, but it retains nothing of the appearance it had when it
withstood a fierce siege from the Hammer of the
Scots.

Balaam was pleased with his outing, our only
serious digression from the sea-route, though he
pretended, as always, to have a grievance.

"No," he said, "I shall never understand. The
natives may have some reason for pronouncing
Glamis as if rhymed with palms, but when you call
Kirriemuir something that rhymes with lums, the
limit has been reached.

> Sing it with psalms!
> We've just been to Glamis.
> Sound it with drums!
> We've dawdled in Kirriemuir. . . .

No, I shall never understand these things."
But I think he understands them very well.
And so back to Montrose and stern duty.

X

TO AULD ABERDON

We left Montrose by the fine coast-road, and not by the inland way towards Laurencekirk, by which Johnson and Boswell travelled to see that queer pre-Darwinian, Lord Monboddo, whose fervent belief was that Man had a tail. (Dean Ramsay tells how he and his brothers, as little boys, hoped wistfully for a sight of the Monboddo tail, but were disappointed.) Boswell feared that the queer old lawyer and the Doctor would quarrel violently, and anxiously watched for the first unhappy spark that would set their conversation into an angry blaze, but, fortunately, they were so opposite as to be able to agree, and Bozzy had the pleasure of seeing them "liking each other better, hour by hour," though the Doctor did afterwards confess that he had done greater feats with his knife and fork than at Monboddo's frugal table.

The farther north you go, the wilder and grander grows the coastline. We crossed the North Esk by a fine bridge, and kept on by the high road, with the railway running below, towards St. Cyrus, which was once called Ecclesgreig, after an early king of Scots—there were many in those days—who embraced Christianity. The road below St. Cyrus might have been specially constructed, not so much as an efficient highway, though it is all that, but as a marine drive for the wandering traveller's pleasure.

Once more there is that perfect colour symphony —red of the ploughland, green of the pasture, blue of the sea. Always down below, is that blue riband of sea, with its lacy edge of foam. We stopped to look down from the road on the tiny village of Johnshaven. It was as though we were gazing from a mountain-top into a bright sea-valley. Sunlight on the red tiles of an odd roof or two added gay colour, and the picture of the fishing village nestling under steep braes might have been deliberately "composed" for the sightseer's pleasure by some skilled artist.

Gourdon is another pretty village, which seems to wander down to its nestling haven in little rows and terraces. Here again the sunlight picked out red roofs among the grey. From the sea it must be an enchanting sight, like a toy town made from a child's bricks, scattered carelessly on the hillside.

The way now grew steeper and the road, instead of following the crest of the slope, was a mountain path curving along at half its height. Green banks rose above the road as steeply as they fell away below. On this sharp slope above the road, we saw half-a-dozen shaggy Shelties, contentedly cropping the grass while they stood, calmly surefooted, at alarming angles to the slope. You would scarcely have thought that a mountain-goat could have kept foothold up there, but the ponies seemed quite happy.

In the field below we watched another of those ploughmen who go down almost to the sea's edge, and also, for the first time, a curious sight that we were often to see again upon the sloping ploughland. At a discreet distance behind the plough-tail marched, or rather hopped, two separate and compact little regiments, one in black uniforms and one in white. The crows and the gulls were having a field-day, but they seemed anxious to show that they had no connection with each other.

Bervie must at one time have been a much bigger town than it is now, for it was made a Royal Burgh by David the Second, who landed there after his youthful exile in France, during the Baliol wars. At Kinneff, a couple of miles farther north, is an old church, beneath whose floor the crown jewels—the Honours of Scotland—were hidden at a time when Cromwell's troopers were doing their best to find them. It was from Dunnottar Castle that the jewels were spirited away into safety, by the skill and address of the Kinneff minister's wife.

When you see Dunnottar Castle from the road, it is apparently tucked under a fold of the fields below, but when you dismount and investigate, you find that it stands out on a rocky peninsula which might have been an island, but for the narrow isthmus across which you pass towards the great square tower and the massive gateway. Dunnottar reminds you a little of Castle Urquhart, but is even stronger. It belonged to that brave northern family, the Keiths, Earls Marischal, who almost always fought gallantly on the losing side. (They were Covenanters at the

DUNNOTTAR CASTLE

"Stands on a rocky peninsula, which ought to have been an island."

time when Montrose's star was in the ascendant, but Jacobites in the unhappy Fifteen.)   This cannot be the castle that Wallace stormed, for its oldest parts were not built till almost a hundred years after Wallace's time, but the position must have been more or less the same, and the hero's scaling of those jagged brown rocks was a feat of unexampled daring. Montrose besieged Dunnottar in vain during one of his whirlwind campaigns, and later Cromwell captured it, but found that the regalia, which he was seeking, had disappeared.   The jewels had been taken to Dunnottar, as the strongest hold in Scotland, but when it was found that the garrison could hold out no longer, a cunning and richly humorous ploy carried the regalia to safety.   This was carried out, as I have said, not by any romantic beauty, but by Mrs. Grainger, the douce good-wife of the minister of Kinneff.   This lady—trust a minister's wife for having a way with her—received permission to pass through the English lines and call upon the governor of the castle.   When she came out, she was carrying an innocent-looking bundle of "hards"—"hards" are unheckled lint, if that makes you any wiser—and in the stems of the hards the jewels were neatly hidden. One story says that the sceptre, an awkward thing to hide, was skilfully disguised as a distaff, with the lint hanging round it in a natural and innocent manner. In any case, honest Mrs. Grainger came out smiling, and the English general, as any gentleman would do to a lady incommoded by parcels, courteously helped her to her horse. With the aid of her good man, she hid them in the floor behind the pulpit of his church, and there they stayed till King Charles came into his own again. There is an alternative story of the jewels being let down from the castle rock and caught in an old fishwife's basket, but, although this tale has its merits, I prefer the other. I cannot resist the notion of the buff-coated Ironside officer gravely handing up the wicked adventuress of the Manse on to her steed.

The road curves down into Stonehaven with a tremendous dipping sweep. You see a little grey-roofed town, set on a bay as sharply carved as a scimitar. Like so many of the Fife burghs we had passed earlier, Stonehaven keeps one eye on the fishing and another on a more modern world of visitors who want sands and links. Thus there is an old fishing town of narrow, crooked streets and queerly-gabled houses, that clings round the harbour, and also a brand-new town, steadily building itself up on the other side of the river, looking as bright and new as any modern holiday-maker could wish. For myself, I have a special delight in queer old havens and fishing quays, but anyone, whatever his tastes, might find pleasure in the long, firm sands of that marvellously curved bay. Stonehaven is the capital of the tiny county of Kincardineshire, called in old times The Mearns. The Howe of Angus lengthens into the Howe of the The Mearns, of which Violet Jacob wrote so exquisitely:

And we'll bide our time on the Knowes whaur the broom stands
    braw
        An' we played as bairns,
Till the last lang gloamin' shall creep on us baith an' fa'
        On the Howe o' the Mearns.

The Men of the Mearns were ever men of stout heart and determination, and such a one was William Burnes, who set out southwards from an impoverished croft to make his fortune. His life was a series of heartbreaking struggles with poverty and ill-health, and he made no fortune. "The men o' the Mearns maun do nae mair than they may. . . ." But he was the father of a lad that was born in Kyle and sang Scotland's sweetest songs. Robert Burns himself once visited Stonehaven, on his last northern tour, and he wrote a characteristic note in his journal: "Near Stonehaven the coast a good deal romantic —meet my relations—Robert Burnes, writer in Stonehaven, one of those who love fun, a gill, a punny joke, and have not a bad heart—his wife a sweet hospitable body, without any affectation of what is called town-breeding." Many a joke, and perhaps many a gill, those two must have had together. . . .

The view of Stonehaven Bay is just as fine when you look back on it from the north as when you approach it from the south—a sickle of golden sand, set in the gleaming blue of the sea. On we went by a road that still sweeps along high above rocky cliffs. There were sheep on the banks above— creatures that were not content to nibble the grass but were pulling in a rather aggressive way at whin-bushes. The sea was still with us, away below on the right; now it was not always blue, but sometimes shot with gleaming shadows—purple, grey and every shade of green.

There is a charming essay of Chesterton's, in which he describes how he arrived at an inn in a village whose name he did not know. No one told him where he was, and yet such a calm and holy atmosphere reigned and brooded there that he felt he must be in the presence of some great unknown. He was right, for the village was Stilton, a name thrice-sacred in the history of cheese.

In just the same way Balaam, when we reached a point of the road about half-way between Stonehaven and Aberdeen, began to display signs of agitation.

"It must be about here," he said, "unless the map is lying."

The map did not lie, and we found the place, but only "wi' deefficulty." We had to leave the car, scramble down steep slopes and cross the railway. No doubt there is a much easier way of finding the spot, but we were too eager in our search to take the right road.

Findon, the authentic and sacred home of the Finnan Haddock. . . . Surely a spot to doff the bonnet and bow the knee.

"I must admit I'm disappointed," said Balaam.

Findon is only a little grey fishing village, hardly distinguishable from any other grey fishing village along the rocky coast. It has given a name to something of national—nay, imperial—importance, and yet . . . nothing has been done to mark the almost holy significance of the spot.

"Well, well," said Balaam, "here's a way to treat a reverent pilgrim. No swinging sign, bearing the arms—a haddock rampant. No granite statue to that historic benefactor of mankind who hauled the first haddock from the vasty deep and smoked it in his own chimney. I shall write to the papers about this. . . ."

Scott has spoken of the Finnan haddock with a rapture that would have shown him to be a poet, even if we had had none of his poetry. "A Finnan haddock, dried over the smoke of the sea-weed and sprinkled with salt water, acquires a relish of a very peculiar and delicate flavour, inimitable on any other coast than that of Aberdeenshire. Some of our Edinburgh philosophers tried to produce their equal in vain. I was one of a party at dinner, where philosophical haddocks were placed in competition with the genuine Finnan dish. These were served without distinction whence they came; but only one gentleman, out of twelve present, espoused the cause of philosophy."

As for ourselves, alas, at Finnan, we were obliged to rest upon our philosophy.

We passed over the fine bridge of Dee and reached Union Street, Aberdeen's great white way, where Balaam, just a year before, had been boarded by

pirates.   If a great modern street wants a model of
how to behave itself with cleanliness, dignity and
that quality which in a person is called "presence,"
I should recommend it to try to look as much like
Aberdeen's Union Street as possible.   Union Street
can be as white and glittering in spring sunshine as
ever Broadway is at night.   The main streets of
modern cities are often neither clean nor dignified,
but Union Street shows how the thing can be done.
On this occasion, however, we were not so much
concerned with modern Aberdeen as with the Old
Town, at which we had not looked very closely
the last time.   While, roughly speaking, modern
bustling Aberdeen lies at the mouth and stretches
northward of the Dee, the Old Town is of the Don,
hence its ancient name of Auld Aberdon.

We turned to the left at the end of Union Street
and made our way along King Street in the direction
of the Brig o' Don.   The Old Town lies on the left
of the road.   "Ther was no citie in Scotland," says
the old chronicle, "which did suffer more hurt than
Aberdeen did, nor oftener," but now it rests from
troubled times and has a peaceful, sedate and slightly
donnish air, such as you might expect to see in the
quiet suburbs of Cambridge.   It was made a burgh
of Barony at the end of the fifteenth century, but it
has a history, partly well authenticated and partly of
charming legend, which stretches far away beyond
that date.   The cathedral of St. Machar is a
specially fitting church for the Granite City, for it is

the only granite cathedral in Britain that is not modern. There was a church here in the twelfth century, but the earliest work we see—there is not much of it—was done two hundred years later and much more was added in the early fifteen-hundreds by Bishop Gavin Dunbar, whose canopied tomb still lies in the south transept. Many of the fine stones were taken away, not, as so often happened, for ordinary building purposes, but by Cromwell's troopers, who were building a fort and knew strong stonework when they saw it.

Who was St. Machar? Legend tells how this good saint was sent forth by the fiery-eyed missionary Columba, to build a church on the wooded height above a river "that wound like a shepherd's crook . . .," and in 1136 David the First transferred hither the see of an earlier bishopric. Thus the symbol of the river, like a shepherd's crook, was given true significance.

On the opposite side of the High Street is King's College, which was the first home of the University, but, apart from the beautiful chapel, the college buildings are not old. It was while dining at King's College that Johnson ate several platefuls of Scotch broth, with barley and peas in it.

Boswell: "You never ate it before."

Johnson: "No, sir; but I don't care how soon I eat it again."

This was the most eloquent testimony to the "scottification" of an English palate.

Founded by Bishop Elphinstone in 1494, the college was rebuilt at various times during the nineteenth century. The crown-tower of the chapel is, I think, the most pleasing sight in Old Aberdeen. Quiet lies here after stormy times—a quiet and charm expressed in the poet's lines:

> Gie me the Auld Toon:
>   For Time wi' his sheerin' heuks
> Devalls at the sicht o' my goon
>   An' my birn o' buiks.
> Gie me the Cauld Toon
>   Wi' its noddin' neuks . . . [1]

The Brig o' Don on the main north road was built by Telford and is of no great age; to see the Auld Brig you must go a little way up the river. The Auld Brig o' Balgownie, set among the trees, raises a high pointed arch over the river. Here Byron would walk, as a boy, and when he looked back on the brighter days that lit his unhappy childhood, the auld brig would loom largely in his recollections:

> As Auld Lang Syne brings Scotland one and all,
> Scotch plaids, Scotch snoods, the blue hills and clear streams,
> The Dee, the Don, Balgownie's brig's black wall,
> All my boy feelings, all my gentle dreams. . . .

There must always have been something sinister in that black wall, for a grim legend haunted it—

> Brig o' Balgownie, wight's your wa';
>   Wi' a wife's ae son an' a mear's ae foal,
>   Down ye shall fa' . . .

[1] J. M. Bullough.

168

BRIG O' BALGOWNIE

"Brig o' Balgownie, wight's your wa';
Wi' a wife's ae son an' a mear's ae foal
Doun ye shall fa'."

Photo by Valentine & Sons, Ltd.

And, because he was an only son, young Byron would lean over it with that mixed feeling of romantic excitement and sheer terror which so often lies at the heart of an imaginative boy.

And now, having said good-bye to Auld Aberdon, we were fairly committed to a road that sped farther and farther north. What a road this is, sweeping on mile after mile, sometimes above ploughed land or sandy links, and sometimes above jagged cliffs at whose foot white foam was beating. And all the time the sea was an amazing blue. We spoke to a ploughman, who paused at the end of a straight furrow and shouted at the gulls which followed him in orderly platoons.

"Ay," he said, "the sea's as blue as a sugar-bag the day, but it's no' a blue sea most o' the time. If you're pitten doon in your wee book that it's aye blue, you'll be makin' a great mistake. She's grey and misty an' no' friendly at all when she's roused. She's blue the day, but I wouldna trust her. She can be an auld deevil when she has a mind."

Well, there was first-hand information from the man on the spot, spoken with a douce caution which would not allow his part of the sea to be over-praised. Others who know this coast well have told me that the intense blue we saw was not a prevailing colour. Even in summer, they said, you will see a soft grey haze over the water. But I have always found "Speak as you find" an honest motto, and whatever the prevailing colour may be, I am constrained to give the "auld deevil" her due. She can be "as blue as a sugar-bag" when she has a mind, and this day, if she never has another, was one of her days.

We left the Ellon road, in order to keep on hugging the coast, and crossed the River Ythan by a handsome granite bridge. The coast here once had its smugglers, but it is now more famous for mussels, which are found in the estuary at low tide.

The ruins of Slains Castle stand, like those of Dunnottar, on a massive rock stretching out over the sea. The earliest castle belonged to the hated Comyns, but later became the property of the Earls of Errol, who got into trouble in the Huntley rebellion and saw their home destroyed. They rebuilt it, however, and it was a modern, up-to-date residence when Johnson and Boswell arrived "just at three o'clock, as the bell for dinner was ringing." The Doctor said it was the noblest castle he had seen in Scotland, but he may have been influenced by the dinner.

It was between Slains and Cruden Bay that a bird from a farm gate ran across our track; a curious creature, like a white turkey. Balaam was so surprised that he almost ran over it. It was a pity, really, that he did not run it down, as it would have made a strange curiosity to bring home, unless, of course, I am entirely ignorant and that white turkeys are as common as black ones.

Cruden Bay was a reminder that we were still

in linkland. We saw an imposing hotel, ten times more impressive than any mediæval castle, with a great battlemented tower, on which we almost expected to see a sentry on the look-out with a niblick over his shoulder.

"The largest nineteenth hole I ever saw," said the irreverent Balaam.

The whole bay—and it is a wonderfully fine one—seems to have been turned into one vast golf-course. The sands are a lovely colour and the links are of a kind to delight even the most exacting and fastidious golfer. I never saw GOLF so plainly written on any locality, even North Berwick or St Andrews.

Before going into Peterhead, we left our road to see what we could find out about the famous Bullers of Buchan. The great Buller, which Boswell said was merely a boiler, is a colossal cañon of cloven rock, into which the sea rushes white with foam. I unhesitatingly agree with Boswell's verdict that it is "somewhat horrid to walk along the edge of it." "Somewhat horrid" is good. But Johnson was not content with shattering his companion's nerves by gambolling about on the rocky edge; he must make the journey into the boiling "Pot" by boat, and make it he did, though the entrance was so narrow that the boatmen had to ship their oars.

Peterhead is as red as Arbroath, but the red is not of sandstone but of fine granite from the famous quarries that lie between Boddam and Buchan Ness.

Peterhead is the most easterly town in Scotland, but Buchan Ness, a little to the south, is actually the most easterly point. Coming into the town by a fine red road, we saw a grand sweep of bay and a fine harbour flanked on the nearer side by a big breakwater. In one part there were little gardens, gay with daffodils, running almost down to the quay, but mostly the quayside did not wear a prosperous look. The main dock was full of fishing boats laid up, waiting for the beginning of the herring season. From Peterhead the boats once sailed to far Northern waters for the sealing and the whaling, but there is no sealing and very little whaling now. The herrings are the thing, though even the herrings "are not so good as they once were." Peterhead, like so many of the fishing towns, has a brave air of enduring hard times with fortitude and good humour, and all must wish such towns the best of luck, for the fishing is a gruelling and dangerous life at the most prosperous of times and it is sad to see brave effort bring little profit.

> When you're sleepin' on your pillows
> Dream ye aught of those puir fellows,
> Darklin' as they face the billows
> A' to fill your woven willows?

The moral of the old song is truer to-day than it ever was, so good luck to the herring-boats and the brave men who sail them! Marischal is still the great name in Peterhead. The fifth earl, George,

Photo by Valentine & Sons, Ltd.

THE BULLERS OF BUCHAN

"A colossal cañon of cloven rock, through which the sea rushes, white with foam."

founded it as a Burgh of Barony and the last earl left it, an exile in the service of the unhappy prince, who landed there to begin the ill-starred adventure of the Fifteen. A kindly haven on a stormy and hospitable shore, and so the Old Pretender found it, but it was not enough to have friends in Peterhead.

Our road now bore us slightly away from the coast, through an expanse of flat cultivated land. At Crimond was written the famous song, Logie o' Buchan, which came from the pen of the Jacobite schoolmaster of Rathen.

> My daddie looks sulky, my minnie looks sour,
> They frown upon Jamie, because he is poor;
> But daddie and minnie although that they be,
> There's nane o' them a' like my Jamie to me.

There is a Burns touch about that.

Between Crimond and the sea is the small loch of Strathbeg, which seems as if it ought to have been a lagoon, but its eastern side, though near to the sea, is closed in. We came out towards the coast along the road below which the picturesquely-named villages of St. Combs, Inverallochy and Cairnbulg run into one another, and kept near the sea until the tall spires of Fraserburgh came into sight.

XI

THE MORAY FIRTH

WE had looked upon Fraserburgh as a special landmark, a corner-point in our coastal journey, for henceforth we should be running westward instead of north. It would be unkind to say that we found the corner-town disappointing. If we found it quiet, that was because we were so ill-judged as to enter the town on early-closing day.

Balaam has sketched out a gloomy vision of a wayfarer in Scotland who, travelling each morning over bare moorlands and arriving every afternoon at the next town on early-closing day, died of starvation on the Sunday. It is a sombre subject, well worthy of a poem in the modern manner, but there is no need for it to be written down yet. We have caught several towns on half-holiday and have not starved up to the present. The point of the early-closing episode is that it should point a moral for those who abuse the Scottish Sabbath. These enlightened folk who dislike the Sabbath are all in favour of that progressive institution, Early Closing, but—and this is my case, as the lawyers say—if the Sabbath makes a town quiet and empty and dull, so does the weekly half-holiday. Well, I am for toleration, like the old, bold mate of Henry Morgan, and, if only from sympathetic laziness, I like to see people having as many holidays as they can. But they cannot have it both ways. They cannot call the Sabbath dull and the half-holiday jolly, for both have the same effect upon the town.

We realised that we must not blame Fraserburgh for its quietude and did our duty by its splendid harbour; by Kinnaird's Head, with its lighthouse built upon an ancient tower; and by the parish church, the fine spire of which we had seen a long way off, but when an old fisherman on the quay told Balaam that in the month of July more herrings were landed at Fraserburgh than anywhere else on the east coast my poor friend began to look hungrier and hungrier. July, his expression said, was a long way off. Even when I informed him that James the Sixth once gave Sir Alexander Fraser permission to found a university in the town, he did not brighten, and he was not in the least surprised to hear that the project fell through.

"I expect the king came up on an early-closing day," he snapped.

A few moments later, he was driving the car savagely westward, with bitter hunger in his heart. He pulled up at a little shore village called Sandhaven and stopped opposite a house, with daffodils in the garden.

"People with such a nice garden as that," he said, "would be sure to have kind hearts."

So he knocked at the door and pathetically begged for tea.

"We're spring cleaning," said the lady who answered his summons, "but would you like to go for a walk for ten minutes?"

We walked for ten minutes on the rocky shore of Sandhaven, where the backs of the houses go down to the sea. A snell north wind, carrying the scent of what seemed like all the seaweed in the world, blew on us unkindly. The sea was cold and grey . . . but only for ten minutes. At the end of that period of soul-testing, we sat down in a spick-and-span little sitting-room, to the most marvellous Scotch tea. Hunger makes all things relative, and no doubt caviare, lobster and pheasant might, under different circumstances, have tasted as nicely as those lightly-boiled eggs, that crisp home-made bread and those delectable cookies. But I doubt it. . . .

"I've said some hard things about Scotland," said Balaam, looking up at the print of Lady Butler's "Scots Greys at Waterloo" which hung above our heads, "but a country that can give grub like this —at ten minutes' notice, to disreputable-looking strangers—is jolly well worth fighting for."

Which was a generous tribute, even if spoken with a mouth full of buttered scone.

"At least," I said, "you ought to apologise to Fraserburgh for the hard things you said of it, because if it hadn't been early closing day in Fraserburgh, you wouldn't have found joy and peace at Sandhaven."

"I'll apologise to anyone," said Balaam graciously. "You won't be needing that odd scone, will you?"

So, here and now, our *amende honorable* is freely given; and we set it down, under our hand and seal, that Fraserburgh is a fine town.

"And if that university had come to anything," said Balaam, "I'd have considered sending my son there, if I'd been married and had a son."

The road was right on the rocky edge of the sea, but now we did not mind the sharp wind that blew up from the firth, or even the highly concentrated scent of the seaweed. Rosehearty is as picturesque as its name, but it did not strike me as Scottish-looking; with its low whitewashed cabins it seemed to be like what I have always imagined villages on the west coast of Ireland to be. At any rate, it is much more foreign-looking than its neighbours. A sunny bright place in spring and summer, but a gey cauld spot in winter, I should say. There is an old story that the Danes landed here long ago and taught the Rosehearty folk the art of fishing, but the tale sounds improbable, because the Danes were more given to robbing and burning than to the gentler art of instruction, and, besides, it is hardly likely that the people of a village that lies right on the shore would have been ignorant of the knowledge requisite to catch fish for dinner.

Still we kept by the sea, along a coast of sharply jutting promontories. After Aberdour, called New

Aberdour, I suppose, to distinguish it from old Aberdour in Fife, we turned sharply inland and indulged in a little gentle mountain-climbing. Our main coast-road had behaved extremely well so far and had done nothing ill-natured in the way of surfaces or gradients. Now, having left the main road, we were gently reminded that we were in the North Countree. Balaam looked at the map and found it well-intentioned but vague; studied a forlorn-looking signpost and found it even vaguer; and then set out on a precipitous downward journey on a slope that grew steeper as we proceeded.

"I don't think this is the right road," I hazarded timorously.

"It must be," said Balaam. "The sea is somewhere at the bottom, and our orders were to keep to the coast, weren't they?"

That was true enough. Our intention had been to hug the coast as tightly as possible from Berwick to John o' Groats. At the precise moment, however, we were not hugging the route; indeed, it was only the excellence of our tyre-treads which kept us from flying off into space. The sea was visible, true enough, but there seemed every likelihood of our entering it as a Carnival punt enters a water-chute. Just as I prepared for extremely unpleasant contact with the Moray Firth, the alleged road took its fortieth-odd sharp bend and ended abruptly in a farm-yard.

"If you tell me that this is the wrong road," said

Balaam, between his teeth, "I shall assault you with a spanner."

I was much too grateful to be alive to indulge in recrimination.

"Don't worry," I said. "I admit the road goes no farther and that the only way out is up the quite impossible hill we've just come down. But do not let that disturb you. Here we are with several square yards of level ground at our disposal. Let us stay here for the rest of our lives, or, alternatively, abandon the car and walk back to Fraserburgh."

The hens in the little stackyard clucked at us disapprovingly and a solitary sheep—the most cynical-looking sheep I have ever seen—put its head over a low stone wall and regarded us with open contempt.

"No," said Balaam. "There's a lot to be said for Safety First, but I haven't driven five hundred odd miles to be sneered at by a sheep."

Whereupon he turned the car, blew a truculent "Sez you" on his hooter at the sheep, and set our bonnet at the bank. The upward journey was "somewhat horrid." (I thank thee, Boswell, for teaching me that phrase.) Indeed, it was somewhat horrider than the previous descent, because the prospects of going over a cliff are not rendered appreciably rosier by the thought that you may go backwards, instead of nose first. However, our engine endured the ill-deserved strain upon it in an exemplary manner and in ten minutes we had noisily chugged to the top of the slope and stood opposite the vague signpost which had led us wrong.

Balaam mopped a brow which was almost as warm as our radiator.

"I can see now," he said, "which was the right road—but you must admit that it doesn't look as much *like* a road as the farmyard one."

For the next hour we abandoned ourselves to what the French call *alpinisme*. We lost faith in our maps. We lost faith in everything except the charmed ability of our small car to climb and descend hair-raising slopes. To this day I have but the vaguest notion of where we were or why we should have been going round in precipitous circles. The map, in its well-intentioned way, told us that we were in the vicinity of Pennan, but for all we saw of that no doubt delightful village, it might have been spirited away by the Silent People Who Must Not Be Named. We were wandering like lost sheep up and down rutted mountain-tracks. Just as it was becoming clear that only a well-trained sheep could save us, we came suddenly within sight of the sea again. It was a wild but heartening sight, a wonderful vista of rocky coast-line, seen from the high road, stretching away to the west and ending in a towering, jagged promontory at the foot of which cottage roofs clustered cosily. At last we were upon a real road again, and within half-an-hour we were going down Macduff's steep main street towards the sea. Macduff lies on a sharply-curved little bay and its street rises steeply backwards from the fine harbour. When we expressed surprise at finding a place named after the Thane of Fife on the shores of the Moray Firth, we were told that the little fishing town had only had that name since the eighteenth century, when it was bought by the first Earl of Fife and made a Burgh of Barony fifty years afterwards by the second. Up to that time it was called Down after the green Hill of Down which looks out to the sea from behind it.

We drove along the harbour road and crossing the old bridge over the Deveron found ourselves in Banff. We had last crossed the Deveron on our previous tour by the bridge that links the road from Keith to Huntly. A good bridge that, though not so fine as this one, with its seven arches, which joins Macduff to Banff.

Of all the towns in this northern region Banff is the oldest and has the stormiest history. Of the castle that a conquering English king once occupied, only a few broken fragments of wall are left. So far north the Hammer of the Scots battered his way, but after the final defeat of Bannockburn, all the English garrisons were completely cut off in a hostile land. Of these the force in Banff Castle was the last to give in. Afterwards it was a Scottish royal residence, and a favourite of many queens.

The Black Bull Inn, where Johnson stayed and

grumbled because he could not open the windows, no longer stands in Low Street. What a perfect Englishman was Johnson! Because the inn-windows at Banff had no pulleys, the anger of the fresh-air fiend was aroused, and he went about to the day of his death saying that no single window in the whole of Scotland would open and that every Scotsman from Macbeth downwards hated fresh air. Similarly, when Balaam and I were in Switzerland, I heard him denounce the entire population of the mainland of Europe—"Frousty blighters to a man," he called them—merely because the catch on the window of his *wagon-lit* happened to be jammed.

Well, the Black Bull, pulleyless windows and all, has gone, nor will you find the house where Byron stayed as a boy. It was in this street, where a fountain now stands, that they erected the gallows-tree, below which Macpherson the outlaw "played a spring" on his fiddle and danced it round, before going to a brave death. When Burns visited Duff House, the entrance lodge of which is nearby, he was shown Macpherson's sword, and the tale of the reiver's gallant and reckless death so gripped his imagination that he wrote "the wild storming song" of Macpherson's Death:

> Sae rantin'ly, sae wantonly,
>   Sae dauntin'ly gaed he:
> He played a spring and danced it round
>   Below the gallows tree.

Duff House is now an hotel and no longer a ducal residence, and part of the grounds, presented to the town by the Duke's munificence, is now a public park.

Somewhere on the road between Banff and Cullen is a spot where Burns, travelling with Willie Nichol, stopped to ask a village lad the way to Duff House. When Nichol asked the boy if he knew that he was talking to a great poet, he showed that the poems had found a welcome in the north. He knew the laughing tale of "Death and Dr. Hornbook" and the rattling dialogue of "The Twa Dogs." "But best of a'," he said, "I liked 'The Cottar's Saturday Night,' though it garred me greet when my faither had me read it to my mither." Instantly Burns's hand was on the boy's shoulder.

"Well, ma callant," he said, "I don't wonder at your greeting when you read that. It garred me greet mair than once when I was writing it at my father's fireside. . . ."

Sweeter than all the encomiums of the Edinburgh critics must the boy's reply have sounded in Robin's ears, for here on this lonely northern road far from Ayrshire, he found that his words had sunk deep into the hearts of the simple folk for whom he wrote.

Portsoy lies on this road between Banff and Cullen and has been renowned for centuries for its beautifully grained marble, which is found in veins of light green and delicate pink. Two of the great ornamental chimney-pieces in the Palace of Versailles are made from Portsoy marble.

Dusk was falling as we drove down the wide main street of Cullen, but the gathering shadows could not hide the quiet charm of the place. Cullen is very old, but bears no trace of the scars of ancient strife. Here, one felt, was the most enchanting little town on the Firth, for here were concentrated all the ingredients that go towards the recipe for making the ideal seaside place: tranquillity, light fresh breezes from the water, streets sloping gently down to the sea, thick woods behind, and—a very important ingredient, this—a great green hill looking down on town and shore in watchful benevolence. Those are the instructions for making the ideal Firthside town and here at Cullen they are perfectly carried out. Under the shadow of the Binn of Cullen, the town lies peacefully. That tall green hill has looked down through the centuries. It knows, though no one else is quite sure, for no stone remains, where stood the castle in which the Bruce's fair queen died. It saw the sacking and burning of the town by the wild Highlanders, whose fierceness the noble Montrose found hard to control, and it saw more clansmen foraging for provisions in the kitchen of Cullen House before disaster overtook them at Culloden. It must, too, have seen the chaise, in which Johnson drove from Banff, "a very good one and very good horses." It is a common saying, "to be as old as the hills," and yet the high Binn, that looks down on ten counties and has seen so much of human strife and heroism and folly, has in its green slopes all the freshness of a charm that never grows old.

We put up at a small hotel bright and clean as a new pin, and discovered that the hunger, which had been so mightily appeased at Sandhaven, was returning, and with this recurring weakness of the flesh our landlady set out to deal briskly and efficiently. The supper she brought would have satisfied half-a-dozen travellers. This good lady, it appeared, was not a native of Cullen, and while she generously admitted that it was a pretty place and really very nice for visitors, she did not attempt to conceal the fact that her heart was in her native Dumfries. Indeed, she did not scruple to maintain that the old Mid-Steeple in Dumfries High Street was a far finer sight than the Binn of Cullen, "any day of the week." When I denied this—and I deny it fervently still—she looked on me pityingly and said: "Of course, an Englishman wouldn't understand the feeling."

At which Balaam, chuckling in his ribald laughter, enquired: "And where do you suppose my friend comes from?"

Whereupon the landlady—a good woman, a kind woman and a mother of bonny bairns—replied in these words: "I couldn't exactly say, but there were some people here last year from Manchester and they had the same kind of accent."

It is the duty of the modern novelist to lay bare the secret recesses of the soul, but there are wounds the lacerating agony of which no pen, however realistic, can describe. An English accent, possibly. We are but human, and all have our faults. But Manchester! . . . Balaam hid his evil head in the sofa-cushions. At last the landlady—I have said she was a good woman—saw my look of pain.

"They were very nice people," she said soothingly. "One of them was an M.A."

Balaam, emerging from the sofa, at last did me belated justice, guaranteeing the Scottishness of my forbears and alleging that I had even once written a book about Burns. Not, I have thought subsequently, that this was in itself a mitigating circumstance, for to write a book about Burns is a mark of presumption rather than honest ancestry. Happily all was well.

"If that's so," said the landlady, "perhaps you'll tell me something. I have a boy—you saw him, playing himself in the garden when you came in. He's a good boy, but he has one fault; he's always bothering the life out o' me to go to the Pictures. I hate these Pictures, taking a laddie's mind off his schoolbooks, and sending him home to fire pistols at you round the dark corners of the stairhead. Well, every time he came to me for sixpence for the Pictures, I just refused him, but a fortnight ago he came to me with a sly-like look in his eye, as if to say: 'Caught ye this time.' 'Mother,' he said, 'you can't refuse me this time. It's a fine film, a grand film.' 'Away with your cowboys and their old pistols,' says I. 'Oh, it's nothing like that,' says he. 'Mother, haven't you always told me Robert Burns was a grand man?' 'The grandest man Scotland ever produced, and buried in St. Michael's kirkyard at Dumfries.' 'Well,' says he, 'you canna refuse me this time, for it's a fine film and a grand film, and it's called The Loves of Robert Burns!' And now will you tell me what I was to say to that?"

I was beaten. Solomon might have thrown up the sponge in like case.

"Just tell me that, now. How was I to explain to a wee laddie that Rabbie, for all his awful on-goings with the lassies, just didn't mean any harm, not any at all?"

There have been infinitely more learned and wiser biographers of Burns than the writer to whom this awful poser was addressed, but the wisest of them has not answered it. How *are* we to explain that he meant no harm?

"And what did you say?" asked Balaam quizzingly.

"Oh, I got out of it," said that true mother. "I got out of it without telling a lie. I just said: 'What's on next week?' And he said: 'It's a grand film, The Terror of Deadman's Gulch'——or some such daftlike name. And I said: 'Come to me for your sixpence next Monday, and if you come back, firing pistols round the stairhead, I'll sort ye!'"

I have always doubted the story in which Solomon solved problems which mothers found too difficult. As if mothers have not always been wiser than any Solomon!

And before she bade us good night, she said, as though she knew best and we did not know our own minds:

"You'll take Finnan haddock to your breakfasts."

XII

MORE MORAY FIRTH

WHEN Doctor Johnson was in Cullen, they set down before him at breakfast "dried haddocks broiled." Boswell ate one, but Johnson was disgusted at the sight of them and ordered them to be removed. If he breakfasted solely on a dish of tea, it was his own fault. I am prepared to go to the stake for the statement that Cullen breakfast-haddocks are entirely delectable. They are not philosophical haddocks, but the genuine Finnan dish.

Before we set off we said good-morning to the Binn and looked at the Three Kings of Cullen, great upstanding rocks at the corner of the bay, not forgetting to take a peep at Cullen House, which stands as high as an eagle's nest on a rock looking down on Cullen Water, and is approached by a bridge of one magnificent sweeping span. We consulted our map with some misgiving, for it warned us that we should have some difficulty in standing by our resolution to keep as near the coast as possible, for the main road soon cuts in towards Fochabers and there is no route that hugs the western end of the Firth as closely as we could have wished. We determined, however, to be beaten as seldom as possible and, on sight of a spire that seemed to be near the sea, we hastened down a pleasant by-lane which brought us out at Port-knockie. Here there is a peaceful little harbour that looks as if it had been hacked long ago out of the solid rock. The skipper of a storm-tossed barque must, as they say, breathe again, when he has steered his boat into the quiet haven of Port-knockie. Away on the right stretches a craggy line of cliffs that reach their most salient point in the fittingly named Scaur Nose. In the opposite direction we found a road, and not a bad one, that would keep us near the sea until we came to Buckie. At Findochty—what a gift-name for a novelist who is going to write kailyard stories of the fisher-folk —the coast-line became less rugged. We were on the edge of linkland once more, where the whole shore could easily be a golf-course if it wished. Findochty is beginning to grow modern and up-to-date in its ways, but Portessie, a mile or two farther along, is what might be termed the real thing; a perfect fishing-village, at least to the artist's eye, its cottages clustering round the crescent bay, as though they were toy houses that a child had grown tired of and thrown down, just anyhow. (Though, of course, no nice child would have grown tired of such attractive toys.)

Buckie, on the other hand, has no need for praise from those who babble of the quaint and picturesque, for Buckie means business. It does not pretend to be a little place of nooks and coves where artists may potter about and do little sketches with an upturned boat in one corner and a crab-pot in the other. No, there is none of that sentimental non-sense about Buckie. Seriously, sternly, almost grimly Buckie sets about the business of providing the fish that you eat for breakfast. Crab-pots, indeed! Do you know Buckie has more real fisher-men—and by real fishermen Buckie means line-fishermen—than any other town in Scotland ? ("Where's your Fraserburgh noo?") On the quay at Buckie Harbour you will see, not the picturesque romance of fishing life, but all the evidence that fishing is a big business and a remarkably well-run business at that. Yes, Buckie means business, and business means breakfast.

It was a little to the east of Portgordon that the wind caught us, a tearing, swithering wind that rushed at us right off the grey Firth. The car rocked on its springs in the force of it and we saw little knots of children being skirled home from school in it, the boys' mufflers and girls' pigtails blowing straight out behind them in the most curious way. Portgordon's main street gave us momentary shelter from the wind and there I entered a druggist's shop, where I purchased choco-lates, cigarettes, postcards, a copy of the *Aberdeen Press and Journal* and films for my camera. As out of this list only the films are technically, if curiously, regarded as drugs, I set this down as a tribute to Portgordon's splendid enterprise and evident desire to do its best for the traveller. Then off we started into the wind again, but the time was approaching when we should have to bid another temporary farewell to the coast. Our road turned inland towards the road-bridge that crosses the Spey just west of Fochabers. Here the railway would have served as a better friend, for the line crosses the Spey by a fine bridge almost at its mouth, but you cannot dump a faithful car at will, when you are motor-touring, for you would soon be condignly punished for your ingratitude. So we left far on our right what looked like a big hotel, surrounded by wide green links with the sea beyond, and hurried south-westwards towards the Elgin road. This is a delightful road, wide, finely surfaced and shaded with beech hedges. (Is any tree lovelier than a beech in spring?). It had even been "improved" since we passed along it in the opposite direction on our journey to Aberdeen last year. A motorist, I suppose, would be hopelessly illogical if he complained of a kindly authority's efforts to straighten out his road for him, but, to the sentimentally inclined, there is something very sad about the little odd bits of road which have been cut out, to make the highway straighter, wider and, incidentally, safer. Once they were part of the proud high road, helping to give it a touch of individuality and character. Now they are shelved for ever, as mere back-waters; pathetic little oddments over which the grass will soon grow.

"Pooh!" said Balaam, who would like all Scotland to be one vast arterial road on which he could scorch without slackening speed once. "You wouldn't say that if I didn't do two-thirds of the driving. Of course it's a good thing to straighten out the road. Look how much quicker you can get there."

"Get where?"

"Wherever you want to go."

"That's just my point. The country is full of lofty hills and smiling valleys, but there is a tendency to dump the hills into the valleys, to make roads to get there. When all the country has been ironed out to make arterial roads to get there, there won't be anywhere left worth getting to."

"You didn't say that when this car was giving its celebrated impersonation of a mountain-goat in the neighbourhood of Pennan," he retorted. "That is, if there really is such a place as Pennan, which I doubt. All this fuss because a couple of dangerous corners have been straightened out. Of course, you can't get anywhere if there aren't any proper roads. You can't have your cake and eat it."

Now that is one of those smug sayings which annoy me intensely. It is by no means necessarily true. The happy life, I maintain, consists of saving half your cake for unforeseen eventualities, and eating the other half with all the joy good cake can bring you. Even if this attitude is illogical, I should still like enough character left on the old roads to make a journey worth while, and that is why I still feel sorry for the little orphan pieces of road which have been cut off and will have no more fun.

This argument brought us to the point where the by-road to Lossiemouth turns off sharply to the right and now there was no further need to argue, for we were heading due northward towards the coast again. A pleasant, friendly little road this, with little fir-plantations by the wayside and the whitewashed walls of neat farms shining through the trees. Presently the country opened out and we saw for the first time a wide expanse of heather-bents, now brown and sad. That is the solitary fault of spring-time; it will give you almost every delight of the countryside, except the wine-red heather in bloom. But . . . who said you could not have your cake and eat it? That depends on the size of the cake, and, after all, we were in the Land of Cakes. If the heather was not in bloom, here at least was the broom, masses of it, oceans of it. There used to be an old Sunday-school hymn which referred rather vaguely to "the golden sea." Here was the true golden sea, rippling in golden waves under the breeze that came up from the Firth. For a symbol of boundless riches and natural careless opulence, commend me to a sea of waving broom. It makes the thought of money-bags seem as mean as money-bags really are.

We came into Lossiemouth by a street where wall-flowers, yellow and red, were growing in the

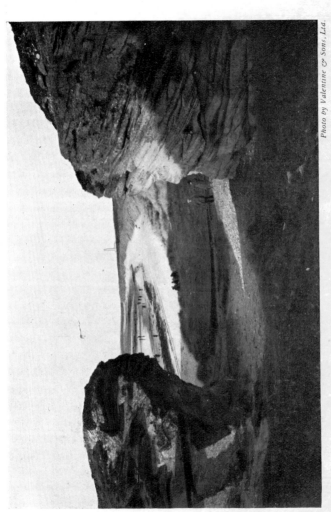

Photo by Valentine & Sons, Ltd.

THE LIGHTHOUSE, LOSSIEMOUTH

"No windswept fishing village, but a thriving seaside resort."

gardens of small grey houses. Lossiemouth was entirely different from the sort of place I expected to find. As the romantic birthplace of a great prime minister, it has naturally received a good deal of attention from the Press, but the impressions given of the place have been somewhat misleading. Perhaps it was wholly my own fault, but I had always pictured Lossiemouth as some bare, windswept fishing village, a place of huddled cottages and forlorn-looking little boats, upturned on the shingle. It is nothing of the kind, which shows, alas, the absurdity of romantically conceived notions. Lossiemouth, on the contrary, is a thriving seaside resort, where the salty breezes blow freshness and vigour, so that when a sadly overworked prime minister flies home, he is not so much re-visiting in sentimental mood the haunts of his childhood as going to one of the best places in this island for his health. So when you drink your premier's health you are really wishing him home in Lossiemouth, where the air is fresher and life is less a matter of meaningless bustle than in London.

I must admit that I did not give up my foolishly romantic notion of Lossiemouth without a struggle. I talked to fishermen and policemen and old ladies in old-fashioned little shops, cunningly working the conversation round to a certain person, but all in vain. They would not be drawn, and even the oldest fisherman would not give me a bite. Not a single person could be prevailed upon to say: "I mind him when he was a barefit laddie," or: "Fancy him, a Lossie Loon, mixin' wi' kings and orderin' all London about." I completely failed to discover any trace of the redoubtable old lady, who, as he has himself confessed, once shook her umbrella at him and said: "I'll no' demean masel by arguin' wi' ye in a public street." My carefully posed questions were fruitless. They knew him and he belonged to them, but that there should be anything out of the ordinary in a Lossiemouth lad's becoming the first citizen of the greatest Empire the world has ever known had never crossed their minds. Romantic? Not a bit. Strange? Nothing strange at all. *If he had a mind to, why not?* That is as far as they were prepared to go.

So I failed, rather disappointingly, to confirm my legend, and had to be contented with the sandy beach and the caller air. Not that the sun always shines in Lossiemouth. While I was talking to my last and most uncommunicative fisherman, a drenching shower began to fall, and I returned to the car to find Balaam being played at by a quartet of melancholy itinerant bandsmen who were wailing out the air, "All Good Pals and Jolly Fine Companee," as though it were the world's last sad pibroch.

"Gentlemen," Balaam was saying to the leader, "without wishing to be personal, I must say that, so far from being jolly fine companee, you are about the worst company I've struck in years."

The orchestra-leader withdrew his cornet from a very red face, which relaxed into the sort of grin whose native home is in the region of the Old Kent Road.

"'Ave an 'eart, guv'nor," said our Cockney Lossie Loon. "'Ere's the ole cornet. 'Ave a dilly at 'er yerself if you think you can do any better."

"No, thank you," replied Balaam politely, "but I'd consider a shilling well invested if it would give us a different tune."

"You don't know what you're askin' for," said the cornet-player. "Strite, you don't. I could give you clarsical stuff myself—the Miserere from You-know-what, and all that—but"—he lowered his voice confidentially—"these other blokes are proper amachures. Got to carry 'em on my back, I have. They only know one other chune, as you might say, *know it.*"

"Let's have it, then," said Balaam, producing his shilling. "It can't be worse than the other."

The band struck up—or rather, fell down into —the most lugubrious ditty mortal ear had ever heard. "It Always Starts To Rain," moaned four different instruments in four slightly, but quite definitely, different keys.

"I told you," said the cornet-player, reappearing from behind his instrument, at the end of the first verse. But that tune put Lossiemouth on its mettle. Lossiemouth, that proud seaside resort, was not going to submit to this indignity for ever. Always started to rain, did it? The rain ceased suddenly, dark clouds parted and a burst of bright sunshine gleamed out over the grey houses, the sands and the sea. Lossiemouth proved definitely that it was not going to be beaten and maligned by a dismal tune. Balaam started his engine, and as I waved a backward good-bye at the corner of the street, our friends were still playing "It Always Starts To Rain," with brilliant sunshine gleaming on their brass instruments.

We followed a wide grey street, where a broad expanse of village-green fronted the church, and passed out on to the shore again, where lay on our right a golf-course that was thickly covered with whins. So that was Lossiemouth. We had found no one who would say: "I kent him when he was a barefit laddie." On the other hand, the last thing we saw in Lossiemouth was a flamboyant poster, promising Talkies in the Town Hall. You cannot, I repeat, have everything in this imperfect world.

The road that took us to Duffus was what Balaam calls a "sort-of" road, but we were grateful to it for allowing us to pursue our journey without turning our backs on the coast and returning to Elgin. The whole of this countryside appears to be sedulously cultivated and well-cared-for, and the black Aberdeen-Angus cattle, grazing in the meadows, had a specially contented air. Through Duffus

[1] For description of Elgin, see *Let's See the Highlands*.

we came to Hopeman, a little grey village, where once more the pleasant tilth goes down almost to the sea, and from there we ran on to Burghead, which looks like a kind of Land's End. We drove up the main street and on to a green headland where the trim white coastguard station stands, looking across the Firth towards the Black Isle. Why do coastguard stations always look the perfection of neatness and cleanliness? At whatever time or in whatever weather you come upon them, they always seem as if they had just "shined up" from doorstep to flagpole, for an Admiralty inspection. I expect the coastguards are mostly old sailors with whom having things shipshape is a natural habit, and even a consuming passion. You would imagine these coastguards were hourly expecting a gale that would blow their whole establishment out to sea, and that they would then be content to sail her, like the good ship she has always been to them, over the ocean in any direction.

Burghead has a very ancient history. The Picts and the Danes both had forts here (which shows their strategic wisdom, for the headland commands a wide sweep of coast, both east and west), and all sorts of odd relics of a Pictish civilisation are dug up here from time to time. The Burghead folk have an ancient ceremonial custom of following a flaming tar-barrel in procession through the streets. They call this "burning the clavie" and say that the flames are intended to drive away evil spirits. I do not know how old the custom is, but I fancy that in the smuggling days it may have been adapted to good local use, not so much by scaring evil spirits away as by keeping the exciselmen occupied at a suitable distance from where good spirits were being safely landed. The only evil spirit we came across in Burghead was the spirit of the wind that seemed to buffet for ever on the lonely headland. It was driving low clouds over the sweep of bay that curves across to Findhorn, and under these scurrying clouds the colours of the Firth were ceaselessly changing through all the shades of green and grey. All the colours that come through the years to weather-beaten slate-roofs in twenty different exposed places were visible in a few moments on the surface of that wind-swept bay. I have never seen such a kaleidoscope.

We turned south again, alongside a railway track that ran over rough sandy links. Here was a lonely little stretch of country, where road and railway looked forlorn, as though they were not quite sure where they were going, but hoped for the best. A patch of rough moorland and then sandy dunes again; so, having crossed the line and left it behind, we came by open moorland, dotted with little spinneys, to the ruined arches of Kinloss Abbey, which has a charming legend of its own. David the First, the "sair saint," was hunting in the neighbouring forest and lost his way. Some say it was a white doe, and others a white dove, which led him from the bewildering thickets into a sweet green glade; whether doe or dove, it was evident to the king that the guidance was heaven-sent, and, with a thankful heart, he vowed that a church should mark the place of the miracle in this holy glade. A monastery was built and the good monks from Melrose came to labour and pray there.

Although we were able to keep near the shore of Findhorn Bay for a little while, we were soon out again on the main road, along which we had passed last year, and passing from Forres through Auldearn to Nairn by a road often shaded by deep fir-woods we made one more effort to find a by-road to the coast. At last we found it and soon came out on the shores of the Firth with the Black Isle lying across the water. This is a quiet road, where the buffeting winds of the Moray Firth do not blow, for now we were on the southern bank of the narrower Firth of Inverness, protected by the headland on which stands Fort George. As you look across the shallow water, you have an illusion of regular bands of colour: first, the grey of the Firth, then the grubby greeny-brown of the tangled seaweed, then a wide flaming stripe of broom that comes down to the shore, and lastly the gentle outline of green slopes beyond. This is a curious freak of colour, turning the landscape into some-thing that looks almost like a long striped scarf. Everything was quiet, as though nothing had ever happened there, or would happen. An old man, sitting by the roadside on the handle of his wheelbarrow, nodded to us gravely and then returned to contemplation and his short stumpy pipe. A pair of yellow-hammers fluttered up from a clump of broom as though anxious to add their pretty share to the colour-scheme. This shore-road, with the Firth on the one side and ploughland on the other, was like a peaceful haven, after the buffeting we had endured on Burghead.

On our way into Inverness we saw one more castle, a great broad-shouldered forthright-looking place, standing up squarely on the right of the road. At first we thought this was Dalcross, but its turrets showed it to be Castle Stewart, once a residence of the Earls of Moray. It was rather refreshing to see so sturdy a house not in ruins, but it has passed through at least one bad gruelling in a seventeenth-century raid by the Mackintoshes.

We came into Inverness by the Kingsmill road, and when we reached the town Balaam suddenly stopped, jumped down from the car and dashed across the road to shake a man in uniform warmly by the hand.

"Who's your friend?" I asked when he came back.

"A splendid fellow," said Balaam, beaming with (for him) rare geniality. "Didn't you recognise him? It's the policeman who cursed us last year."

XIII

THE SECRET OF THE BLACK ISLE

We crossed the bridge over the swift-flowing Ness and, passing the football-ground and the ships at the end of the canal, followed the Beauly road westward, partly along the shores of the Beauly Firth and then inland to Lovat Bridge, the point to which we had once come down green Strathglass after our enchanted journey to Glen Affric. It was a cruel temptation to turn off to the left, for if there is one place that calls insistently it is Glen Affric, of the craggy steeps, the roaring falls and the wild deer. But duty called us northward, past Beauly, the fair place with its ruined abbey among the ancient trees, towards Muir of Ord, where the main road goes on to Dingwall.

Muir of Ord is a bare place, where the most intimate signs of humanity that we could see were the goal-posts of a football pitch. Have you ever thought what those goal-posts mean? We talk rather lightly of the Empire on which the sun never sets, of trade following the flag and other entirely well-intentioned but rather vague platitudes, but to me the most finely symbolic flag is a corner-flag and the truest and noblest outpost of Empire is a goal-post, and when I see those posts in outlandish parts, even if they only have old rope instead of a cross-bar, I feel the thrill of Empire. Goal-posts and all that goal-posts imply are the modest insignia of the mighty British *imperium*. A small thing, compared with proud flag-waving and noisy talk of making-thee-mightier-yet, but how much more the goal-posts mean! I once read a book by a very bitter (and rather childish) anti-Imperialist, who gnashed his teeth when he saw British post offices in Morocco. What would he say if he had seen, as I have seen, goal-posts in France, in Germany, on the edge of the veldt in South Africa, on the plains of India and on the banks of the Tigris? For I, who never thought to wave a flag, become a good Imperialist when I see those posts, for they show that not only in the Empire but over the wider world, British sportsmanship, British fairplay and, above all, British good-temper, have gained a footing, from which heavy guns will not dislodge them.

All of which is a tedious digression; an unfair one, too, if it leads you to suppose that Muir of Ord is some wild hinterland, on the bare outposts of civilisation. On the contrary, it should be regarded as blessed above other villages, for it stands at the portal of the magical Black Isle.

"Are we right for the Black Isle?"

"Ye're on the Black Isle road now."

In considering the Black Isle, you must disabuse your mind of any impressions, however delightful, that the words have first called up. The Secret of the Black Isle . . . It suggests a tale of buried treasure and doubloons and palm-fringed reefs and Jolly Rogers in the good old Stevensonian manner.

A cheering and attractive thought, but quite misleading. The first thing you must learn of the Black Isle is that it is not black and that it is not an isle. The map, which tells the bare truth and has no sentimental illusions, will show you that it is an unostentatious peninsula, lying between the Beauly and Inverness Firths on the south and the Cromarty Firth on the north. But while a map may be trusted to tell you the truth, it does not tell you the whole truth. Assuredly it does not reveal to you the secret of the Black Isle. Even the geography-book reasons for calling it the Black Isle are not very convincing. They call it an isle, because, at the point where it joins the mainland, it narrows to a strip which may be considered unimportant. They call it black, because, at a time when all the rest of the country lies in the iron grip of winter, no white mantle of snow ever lies there. But do not believe that it is really black; when we saw it in spring, it was green with meadows and golden with broom.

We turned to look back at majestic Ben Wyvis, the whiteness of the snow on whose summit made the clouds look murky, and then drove slowly along the Black Isle road. It takes a little time for the enchantment of the Isle to work upon your spirit. Here are no frowning mountains, for we leave Ben Wyvis behind; no gleaming lochs, no foaming cascades, but just a green and tranquil countryside, where the plum-blossom glows white in little sleepy orchards and black cattle stand knee-deep in rich green meadows. The air fell on our cheeks like a caress. The warm breeze among the birch-leaves softly whispered: "Don't hurry, don't hurry . . . don't hurry." The true secret of the Black Isle is that no one who goes there ever wants to leave. There are a hundred spots in Scotland more striking and more magnificent, but none that have that same air of sleepy enchantment. What is there for the traveller to see? Nothing very much. For those who have looked on Loch Lomond or Glen Affric, hardly anything at all. Only a few grey-roofed farms, a little copse or two of silver birch-trees, decked in their fairy tracery of new-born leaves, a group of lazy-looking cows drinking from a duck-pond, and, below the meadow-slopes, the limpid Firth, in "such a tide as, moving, seems asleep. . . ." Nothing exciting or especially romantic. A farm-servant passed us, with a dog sedately trotting at his heels. (I don't think we saw a man on the Black Isle without his attendant dog. It seems to be a place where men and dogs naturally understand one another.) A partridge whirred up from under our wheels; not in sudden panic, but simply and politely getting out of our way, as who should say: "After you, gentlemen . . ." Even the crows and gulls that followed inevitably at the plough-tail seemed friendly and hopeful gleaners rather than predatory bandits. If you tell me that this is sheer nonsense and that gulls are just as greedy here as anywhere else, I will reply that you may be right but that you have never experienced the enchanting illusion of the Black Isle. Here everything seems gentler and kindlier—even the sparrows are less perky and ill-mannered—and if the whole atmosphere is an illusion, then it is the strongest spell I have ever fallen under—an illusion more pleasing than truth.

We just "daun'ered" along. Even Balaam did not feel his usual urge to speed. Still nothing exciting appeared in view. A dainty little farm, a corn-field of springing green swaying under the lightest of breezes, a birch-spinney on a green knowe and a white horse pulling a heavy wain, a football-field with a team of young Aberdeen-Angus bullocks lined up in the centre as though they were about to start a rousing game, a glimpse of a thatched roof seen through a woodland screen of feathery beech-leaves. All these are common things and not such stuff as dreams are made of. Why, then, should they build up such a picture of tranquillity and perfect content? It can only be that they are all tinged by the strange magic of the Black Isle, where the wayfarer loses all sense of time and distance and only knows that he is well content to be where he is.

We came once more in sight of the placid Firth, with a darkly wooded promontory stretching out beyond, and then slid almost imperceptibly into a pleasant village street. Balaam got out of the car and ran forward to speak to a soberly garbed minister who was standing by the roadside. I saw the two of them conversing in what seemed extremely lively pantomime, but when my friend returned, he wore a puzzled expression.

"A nice man," he said, "and scrupulously polite, but mentally afflicted. I asked him the name of the village and all he said was 'Ouch'!"

"Ouch?"

"Ouch. That's all he would say. Just as if he had a pain. Very sad. And a clergyman, too."

"I don't suppose that's what he really said. It hardly seems likely."

"Ouch. Do you think I could have invented a word like that?"

I went into the post office, and, making further enquiries over a friendly postage-stamp, received enlightenment.

"Well?" demanded Balaam as I came out.

"The name of the village is Avoch, but the local people call it 'Auch.'"

"What?"

"Auch. It's not a bit like 'Ouch' when you say it properly."

"Oh, well, have it your own way. It's a pretty little place and I won't quarrel with it, but I think the unsuspecting traveller ought to be warned."

Down among the net-posts on the edge of the pretty little harbour, a crowd of bonnie bairns were playing at shops with bunches of primroses as merchandise. We travelled slowly along the edge of the sea-wall with the water on one side and little cottage gardens on the other, crowded with clumps of sweet-scented wall-flowers. High above us was a steep cliff on whose face a sturdy whin-bush flamed out golden against the bare stone. Ahead lay the quiet waters of the wide sound.

I do not know how far it is from Avoch to Fortrose, for miles seem to mean very little on the Black Isle. The village itself is not so appealing as Avoch, but the setting is lovely, with high red cliffs above, and smooth green fields curving down the lower slopes. If you follow the lane that turns from the old and broken village cross, you will find the shattered walls of the old Cathedral. It seems strange to come upon a Cathedral in this out-of-the-way spot, but it was a very great church once, and the old Bishops of Ross administered their diocese from Fortrose. It was founded in the thirteenth or fourteenth century on the site of one of the very earliest churches in Scotland. Part of it was completed much later by a famous abbot, who had once been a monk at Melrose. There is a curious canopied tomb, set in one of the remaining walls, which bears traces of the image-breakers' hammers. Cromwell is blamed for having carried away its finest stones to build his "Sconce" above Inverness, but I am not certain that this is true. Kinloss is more likely than Fortrose. In any case, if Cromwell was responsible for all the evil deeds with which he is credited, he must have been an over-worked man. My own opinion is that he was far too good a soldier to waste his time in meaningless acts of vandalism, and that tradition has used the word Cromwell, just as we use the word Bolshevik, as a convenient peg on which to hang a good honest general dislike. Montrose destroyed far more places in Scotland than Cromwell ever did, but Montrose has always had "a good press" from the historians. No doubt the attractiveness of his character deserved this, but I do not see why Montrose's nobility should always be an excuse for the general blackening of anyone who happened to be on the other side.

From Fortrose the road runs on to Rosemarkie, and here the traveller must hurry, if he is to go past at all, for, if he pauses for but one good look, then Rosemarkie will have him and it is all over with the poor man. Let me give this solemn warning: Flee from Rosemarkie, as you would flee from a dark-eyed enchantress, lest like True Thomas you should be lost to the world and spend seven years in Fairyland. Not long before, I had attempted to set down Dirleton as the most beautiful village in Scotland, and Balaam, while admitting its merits, had countered by saying it was so very English. Well, Dirleton needs no praise from me, but there is something in what Balaam says. A stranger might easily be excused for saying of Dirleton: "How English!" Of Rosemarkie he would be pardoned for saying: "How charming!"

Now charm is to-day the most villainously over-worked and ill-used word in the language. It is

ROSEMARKIE

" Where a young poet in love might wander with the princess of his dreams . . . "

used to describe practically everything in the modern world from film-stars to fruit-sundaes, from bungalow-sites to bath-salts. Yet it once had a meaning and a good meaning. It has fallen into the wrong hands, because it is such a good-natured, friendly sort of word, and because (herein lies its charm) it stands for all the other words you cannot think of at the time. So when I say that Rose-markie has charm, you will understand that it has a charm quite different from that conjured up in full-page advertisements by film-stars or their favourite bath-salts. It is something that holds out hands to you and begs you to stay. Is it the charm of tiny red-and-white cottages, stretching in a crescent above the sea? Is it the charm of little rock-gardens, covered with trailing aubretia and flanked by close-trimmed holly-hedges? Is it the steeply-wooded gorge that rises behind? Whatever may be the enchantment of the Black Isle, the true heart of it lies round about Rosemarkie. There is a sort of sleepy, cosy lovableness about the village that, search as you will, you will not find in grander places. Those grander places are for other people, but Rosemarkie, you feel, is for you; not the every-day you, that does sordid things like eating mar-malade for breakfast and jumping on buses, but the inner, secret you, that is something of a hero and something of a poet. Yes, if I knew of a young poet who was looking for somewhere to spend his honeymoon with the princess of his dreams, I should send him a telegram bearing the single word "Rose-markie." He would never trouble to reply, of course, because perfect bliss is a supremely selfish state of mind. Years and years later the happy couple would be sitting at the window of their little red-and-white cottage and the poet's wife—a very beautiful woman, as I see her—would say: "You know, dear, you really ought to write to that friend of yours who told us to come here; a queer, ugly man, but you must admit he was capable of having nice ideas."

And the poet would reply: "I know, darling, but what with writing poetry and trimming the holly-hedges and being in love and watering the aubretias and seeing that the children don't fall into the water, one simply hasn't the time for letters. You know how it is."

They would never write, but I would know where to find them—and their grandchildren—any time I wished. That, at any rate, is how I see it. . . . And this information (or warning) is handed on to all young poets who are about to marry.

The road through Rosemarkie encircles the village in a neat loop and swings inland, rising above a steep slope, thick with trees. Then we saw primroses. We had not been so fortunate with our primroses on this journey. Our previous road that wound along the west coast had been literally a primrose path, but the primrose is timid and shy and prefers to hide away from snell winds. But here, where it would seem that "never wind blows loudly," were banks of primroses, rising tier on tier. Up till then we had only seen them in tiny clumps, scattered among the deeper yellow of the broom or the gold of the whin, but here they grew lavishly in God's plenty, thickly clustered on the steep slopes like constellations in a bright sky.

Balaam stopped the car at the top of the hill, to watch a very small child chasing a very large cow in the field below. Balaam wanted to bet on the result of the contest—he was for the cow and I was for the little boy—but no money changed hands, for the exciting race ended in a dead heat, cow and child entering the byre, neck and neck, at full gallop. We lay back and laughed outrageously at the sight of the stern contest; it seemed to be the sort of midsummer night's dream comedy that happened naturally in the Black Isle. Afterwards the little boy, who turned out to be a little girl, came and sat on the gate and told us she had seen a far grander car than ours pass along the road the day before yesterday. Then, lest we should be utterly cast down by the thought of grander (and yellower) equipages than ours, she tied a bunch of primroses to one of our headlamps.

"Though, mind ye," she said, as though unwilling to be complimentary at the expense of strict truth, "the other one would still look grander nor your one."

The road that drops down into Cromarty circles

round a steep brae, so that you see the little town on the bay several times before you enter it. Looking westward, we could make out the grim grey outlines of battleships lying in the Firth opposite Invergordon. On our way down the hill, we stopped to offer a lift to an old lady who was resting against the bank. Very sensibly she had tied her big basket behind her shoulders, which seems much the best way of carrying that sort of load. But she smilingly evaded all our efforts to inveigle her into the car.

"I just wouldna bother you," she said with firm courtesy.

I suspect she was feeling that her basket would be safer on her own strong shoulders than in our dilapidated vehicle, with the dust of at least ten Scottish counties upon its wheels.

Those wheels of ours as we drove down into Cromarty, would have made a fascinating geological study for Hugh Miller, Cromarty's greatest son, and uppermost on our rims were fragments of the old red sandstone he studied so lovingly. Anyone who has read Hugh Miller's *My Schools and Schoolmasters* or *The Old Red Sandstone*, will be constrained to linger long in Cromarty. Miller's life, though it ended sadly under a mental cloud, was a shining example of the triumph of courage and character over poverty. The guiding principle that steered him through every imaginable difficulty was the unshakable belief that knowledge is within the reach

Photo by Valentine & Sons, Ltd.

CROMARTY

"A tiny red town on a little promontory . . ."

of the humblest seeker and that knowledge is power
—the only power worth having. There was about
him something of the rugged forthrightness of a
Cobbett. "My advice to young working men
desirous of bettering their circumstances and adding
to the amount of their enjoyment, is a very simple
one. Do not seek happiness in what is misnamed
pleasure; seek it rather in what is termed study.
Keep your conscience clear, your curiosity fresh,
and embrace every opportunity of cultivating your
minds . . . Learn to make a right use of your
eyes: the commonest things are worth looking at,
even stones and weeds, and the most familiar
animals. . . . If all your minds were cultivated,
not merely intellectually, but morally also, you
would find yourselves, as a body, in the possession
of a power which every charter in the world could
not confer upon you, and which all the tyranny or
injustice of the world could not withstand." That
was the advice of a working quarryman who became
one of Scotland's greatest geologists.

In the main street, by the shore, still stands the
little cottage where Hugh Miller was born. His
father was a sailor—one of the best that ever sailed
the Moray Firth—who went down with his sloop
and all hands in a terrible tempest that swept the
whole East Coast, when little Hugh was only five.
He tells how every day he would climb the green
brae behind the cottage, to look wistfully out for
the sloop with the two squares of white and the

two square topsails. But months and years passed, and the white stripes and square topsails never came back.

He learned his first lessons in a queer little village schoolhouse, by the shore, where the herring-boats as they sailed into harbour could be seen from the windows, and where, as an added attraction, the squeals from the pigs in the slaughter-house nearby often drowned the droning voice of the dominie. He joined with his school-fellows in what must have been the most exciting alarums and excursions that ever interrupted dull workaday lessons. It was a strange ancient custom that the Ross boatman who traded with Cromarty should owe a customs due of twenty peats per boat to the grammar school. If the skipper of any boat attempted to evade this just duty, then the boys, with their master's full per-mission, would make it their duty to dash out and commandeer the right number of peats, or, in default, a spar or boathook as hostage. However intent the class might be on its Latin, a boy had only to say: "Peat-boat, sir!" to give the signal for a deter-mined foray. Under cover of an artillery section, armed with pockets full of stones, the raiders would gallantly board the peat-boat, and secure their lawful perquisites, or, if that were impossible, at least some spar or piece of rigging which could afterwards be triumphantly hung in the rafters of the old school-house, trophies of joyous adventure. Great days!

We wandered on the shore by the red sandstone

harbour, where Hugh, as a child, played at soldiers with coloured shells drawn up in line of battle. The other boys laughed at him for playing with shells, just like a lassie; they did not know that he was marshalling brigades of infantry or charging the square at the head of his dragoons. We looked out over the tangle of seaweed, where at low tide, the boy would trot at the heels of his sailor-uncle, a grave serious man who would discuss the comparative intelligence of the crab and the lobster and show the lad the strange wonders of the shore— the lump-fish, the sea-mouse and the cuttle-fish, which flings out an inky cloud on the faces of its pursuers.

We saw something, standing on the beach, which Hugh Miller's Uncle Sandy, who fought under Nelson at the Battle of the Nile, never lived to look on: a line of cruisers, low and menacing in the water, steaming back from gunnery practice in the open sea and hauling their battered target behind them.

Of the score or so of people we saw walking the streets of Cromarty, more than half were hale old men. Is there something in the climate of the Black Isle that brings about such hearty longevity? Certainly I have never seen in one small place, so many elderly folk who seemed free from the feebleness of age. Normally one pities old age as a thing of pathos and lost dreams, but these white-bearded old gentlemen of Cromarty had the bright eyes of boys.

modest pretensions to know anything whatever about the matter.

"Holly-hedges and rock-plants?" he jeered. "Why, you've never *seen* the Black Isle. When I was there, every hedgerow from Cromarty to Conon was a mass of trailing dog-roses. You never saw anything like it. Aubretias? If you'd seen those wild roses, you wouldn't mention the word." Which is only one more piece of evidence concerning the insidious witchery of the Black Isle.

As the motoring notices say, *you have been warned*.

XIV

MR. BALAAM TAKES TEA

WE drove on to the main road again at Conon, a village which an enthusiastic writer has called the prettiest in the Highlands. I am not prepared to go quite so far as that, but I would certainly award Conon high marks for its charming outlook and for its position at the end of a pleasant green strath on the banks of the rapid river across which Hugh Miller once swam upon a certain exciting occasion. Over the strath a court of high hills looks down, with snow-crowned Ben Wyvis as its king. This bulky giant dominates the whole landscape here just as Ben Nevis dominates the country round about Fort William. It has no spectacular Matterhorn-ish peak, but you can gauge its immense bulk by the fact that however far you travel from it, it scarcely seems to grow any smaller. Other hills, which looked so high, recede into their true perspective as mere spurs, but Ben Wyvis, massively unheeding, remains undiminished in its strength. Hugh Miller gives a vivid account of his swimming the higher reaches of this rushing river at a time when it was in flood. In his 'prentice days he was setting out to begin a building job which lay on the far side of the Conon and, by making a detour, missed the bridge. There was no way of getting across except by swimming, and he was obliged to start his swim encumbered by his chief courage. When we heard that he was dead, we did not believe it for a moment. The papers might say so, but what did the papers know? We boys knew better. When the Russo-Japanese War came along—we were pro-Japanese to a boy, because the Japs were little fellows—and we heard strange, whispered tales of a mysterious Japanese general, braver than all the others, we knew . . . To some it might be a mystery, but it was no mystery to us. It was our Fightin' Mac in disguise and none other. All honour, then, to Dingwall for the honour it has paid to the boyhoods' hero of a generation which grew up to meet, on the threshold of manhood, a war that could not be fought with bare fists.

(In Dingwall there is also a picture palace, to which Mr. Balaam once took a sweet Highland lady, the mother of a large and handsome family, for the purpose of witnessing her first Talkie. It was a solemn occasion, but what that lady thought of the Talkies and how Balaam drove her and her family home in a rainstorm that made the road and the Cromarty Firth scarcely distinguishable—that, as the chroniclers say, is another story. Some day books may be written about it, but for the moment my lips are sealed.) As you leave Dingwall, you must look out for a sharp right-turn by which the road goes on to far John o' Groats. Otherwise, you will go on to the old-fashioned inland watering-place which is called Strathpeffer. You will not thank me for the warning, because Strathpeffer, believe me, is a much nicer place than John o' Groats. It is like a tiny Harrogate, neatly deposited at the foot of Ben Wyvis. It nestles in a pleasant wooded valley, just as Pitlochry nestles under the brindled hill of Ben-y-Vrackie. Here you may breathe mountain air without going to the trouble of climbing the mountain, and no one will force you to drink the sulphur water unless you wish. (Balaam, who knows Harrogate well, maintains that a sulphur water-cure is infinitely more evil than any known ailment from which the human frame might conceivably suffer.)

But if John o' Groats is your goal, you must sternly put aside the temptations held out by mountain air and by sulphur water (if any) and take that turn to the right, which the unwary might miss. We drove along a road that skirts the north shore of the Cromarty Firth so closely that you imagine you are going to shoot into the water at the next corner, and lingered a little in the pleasant village of Evanton, where works the handsomest blacksmith in Scotland. Between Evanton and Alness is another temptation to stray from the coastal route, for there a road rises, traversing a wild moorland region, which local people call the Struie. This cuts off the whole of the peninsula on which stand Invergordon and Tain. We returned later, on our homeward journey, by this road. Except in the region of the Moor of Rannoch, I do not think I was ever on a lonelier road. I have read that on this road there is a

P

tained in the ancient traditional story of the two stout Tammas Tamsons, one of whom had unfortunately passed away.

("Tammas Tamson's deid."

"Fat Tammas Tamson?"

"*Fat* Tammas Tamson."

"Ay, but *fatten* fat Tammas Tamson?")

It must be regretfully recorded that we could not prevail on anyone in Aberdeenshire—not even a country policeman—to talk to us like that. One good cottage-lady did say to Balaam: "*Far* d' ye come frae?" But that *far* was as far as Aberdeenshire would go for us.

Inverness, to the casual hurried observer, has very little dialect. (We listened to two old gentlemen talking Gaelic in Academy Street, but it would be sacrilege to call the Gaelic a dialect.) Ross-shire seems to have even less. There is a curious lilt, a pleasant slow intonation, as though the person had learnt English as a foreign language, from the best authors, and learnt it very well. And that, I suspect, is how English really was learnt in the North. In a country family you may find that the grandfather speaks hardly anything but Gaelic, that the father knows Gaelic well, while the young folk only know an odd word or two. But no one seems to speak anything that is the equivalent of the dialect of a South Country village. So I find it impossible to reproduce the speech of our farmer passenger in its true form. You cannot write down the fascinating lilt of a Highland voice, unless you have the skill, which I have not, of setting it to music.

"Yes," he said, "I know every bend of the road. If you had turned to the right over the railway you would have come to Fearn. You will have heard of the old abbey there. That's where young Patrick Hamilton was abbot before he saw the light. They burned him at St. Andrews, because he loved his Bible, in the year fifteen hundred and twenty-eight. You may be glad you did not go out there past there to Portmahomack, for it is not the best of roads. It is good farming land here, though not so good as in the Black Isle."

There were odd patches of thick woodland by the roadside, but the rest of the land seemed beautifully cultivated. We set down our farmer by the queer old tower in the main street of Tain.

"Very much obledged," he said, as he left us. "If you have the time, go and see Patrick Hamilton's monument in the church. Burned at St. Andrews in the year fifteen hundred and twenty-eight, because he loved his Bible. Thank you awfully kindly, gentlemen."

Tain has been described as a "raw-boned" place, but it hardly deserved that adjective. Small Scots burghs often lack that appearance of cosiness that you find in English country towns—they are usually built of ruggeder stone, and you miss the friendly thatch or mellowed tiles—but Tain is no more gaunt in appearance than most of them. We were grateful to our farmer-friend for telling us about the church, which is worth seeing for its windows alone, especially the beautiful old window at the east end. The Regent Moray, Mary Queen of Scots' half-brother, gave Tain church its oak pulpit—an act of devotion in a life not especially noted for piety.

We came out through Tain to find the low road that swings to the left along the southern shores of the Dornoch Firth. Over the other side we could see the high roof of Dornoch Cathedral, but we had many long Scots miles to traverse and many a game of hide-and-seek to play with the railway line along the low shore before we could reach the town. If, looking up this Firth on a spring morning you could forget for a moment where you were, you might imagine yourself to be gazing on some stretch of Loch Lomond. Cloud-shadows danced on the surface of the still water and little tongues of dark green woodland jutted out into the Firth, sharply silhouetted in the clear light as though the trees had all come out of a Noah's ark. There were ridges of low, rounded hills rising gently in green slopes around the head of the Firth, and higher mountain masses, craggy and even snow-capped, standing up boldly behind. The sky darkened. Heavier clouds were casting black shadows on the water. The heads of the mountains slowly disappeared into the mist. An air of desolation fell on the patches of broken bracken by the roadside. The feathery foliage of the young firs, which had looked like lace-work in the sunlight, now looked cold and stiff.

It was worth while losing the sun for a few moments, for the pleasure of seeing it smile out again. The dark clouds rolled away up the valley towards the mountains. Blue sky showed in bright patches that grew bigger and bigger every minute. The water of the Firth became clear and limpid again. The mountains were still hidden in cloud, but the low knowes glowed with an emerald light. The green of those hills, when the sun kissed them and was friends again, was as rich a colour as any you would find in the Western Highlands. This was a road where travellers less stern of purpose might have dallied all day, watching the play of light and shadow on the water. Sauntering through the tiny oddly-named hamlets of Easter Fearn and Wester Fearn and passing the turning where the road climbs steeply back over the Struie, we came by Ardgay to Bonar Bridge. The Struie frowns down steeply on the Firth road which runs along at its foot.

We had lunch in Bonar Bridge at a little café where we could look out on the river, which, winding down the quiet green strath, runs into the Firth. If we had not wished to look out on the river, there was plenty in the room to interest us, not merely on the table but on the walls. I never saw so many portraits of Burns in one small room before—Burns turning up the mountain-daisy, Burns finding the field-mouse, Burns bidding farewell to Highland

231

Mary, Burns reciting his poems before the quality in Edinburgh.

"It kind o' reminds people," said the landlady. "Just think of all the grand folk sitting, listening to him, and him that had never put foot on a carpet before. That's Dr. Blacklock there. I like him the best o' them. He was blind, you see, but that didn't prevent him from seeing just how great a man Rabbie was. . . . You'll find Bonar Bridge a bonny place, but it's not just as interesting as at the whale time."

"Whale time?" ejaculated Balaam.

"Have you never heard of the whales at Bonar Bridge? I thought everybody knew about that. I mind it well. They came up the Firth and couldn't get out again, poor beasts, because it was too shallow, and there they lay and died on the shore below the bridge. It was a nine days' wonder, and what with the whales and the newspaper men—some of them from London—the place wasn't like itself. There were some that said it was a judgment on the place. Because of the smell the dead whales would make, you see, they feared we would all be poisoned. There's always some, when anything by-ordinary happens, that'll say it's come as a judgment on other folks, but I think better of the Lord myself than that, though, I'll admit, it must have been a bit of a scunner for them that had never believed in Jonah till then. However, people came up from the Government and cut them up and took them away within a week, so nothing awful happened after all. Still, you'd have found it very interesting if you'd been there. You'll be going to John o' Groats, very likely?"

We admitted that we were.

"I've never been myself, but that's where the Americans go. They *will* go, and when they come back, they always look in here, and until they've had their teas, they seem kind of annoyed with me —as if it was my fault!—because John o' Groats isn't more interesting. It's a very cold place, the Americans say. You'd much better take the road up to Lairg. That's a bonnier road. But no doubt you'll please yourselves."

It was with difficulty that I drew Balaam away. Anything really large impresses a journalist, and Balaam was mightily impressed by the tale of the whales. He would have stayed and talked whale with the very companionable old lady for the rest of the afternoon.

The road lies on the shore again, this time on the northern side of the Firth; a pretty road where there is always something to see; little humpy hills, long stretches of still water, banks of primroses and clumps of golden broom among the green, all their colours soft and fresh under a sunlight that is bravely fighting its way through the cloudbanks. This is a road where an artist, if he did not want his colours too bright, would find delight in a myriad soft tints and melting shades. There were little glens on

233

lighthouse. (I should like to train all such very large monuments to be lighthouses.) It is a statue of the first Duke of Sutherland, executed—if executed is the right word—by Sir Francis Chantrey.

We came into Golspie, a village of one long street with a bend in the middle and left it by a queer crooked old bridge, which might fittingly have been discovered on the road of the old woman in the nursery rhyme who found a crooked sixpence beside a crooked stile. Dunrobin Castle stands back from the road, and looks down towards the sea on the other side. You pass one of the big lodge gates and catch glimpses of turrets and gables through the trees. The glimpses you catch are "baronial" glimpses; that is to say, the towers and turrets that you see are mostly mid-nineteenth-century additions and not the great keep which was built by the second Earl of Sutherland six hundred years before. Past the castle, the slopes below the road are full of green woodlands and little glens, enchanting in their mystery. From the wood a gorgeous-hued cock-pheasant flew right across our windscreen. Then the road swung back to the sea again. Looking back along the coast we could still see the distant lighthouse on Tarbat Ness.

At Brora we met a group of girls carrying fish-creels. Not long afterwards we paused to look down from the shelf along which the road winds, at the sandy links and the rocks upon their edge. The railway is far below, almost on the edge of the sea, and seems to wander in and out of a succession of little sandy bays, where the sea-weed lies in long dark stretches at low tide. The afternoon sunlight danced and shimmered on the sea and, except for a lone swooping sea-gull, not a living creature was in sight. The contemplation of so wide an expanse of salt water made Balaam feel thirsty, and, taking our kettle and primus, we clambered up the green bank into a little hollow, where our stove might be boiled without interference from the wind. While the kettle boiled, Balaam lolled luxuriously on the grass. The sun, the fresh air, the sea view and the first cigarette for a couple of hours all seemed to combine to produce in my friend a feeling of philosophical contentment.

"This," he said, "is undoubtedly the life. We haven't seen a human being for half an hour. I look with just suspicion on all high-flown chatter about the open road and the wind-on-the-heath-brother. The people who talk most about that usually travel in charabancs to seat forty. But to find a really lonely spot by the sea is a genuinely fine achievement because it enables one to get away from that singularly unpleasant bunch, one's fellow-creatures."

"I like my fellow-creatures quite a lot," I objected.

"That," said Balaam, "is mere mawkish sentimentality."

"But I do, honestly. I know liking your neighbour is a duty, but I sometimes think that if no

XV

MR. BALAAM SLEEPS OUT

Portgower is a little line of low white-washed cabins perched on the edge of a cliff, with the railway running on the sea's rocky edge far below. Here Balaam, who can do everything better than everyone else in the world, discovered an aged man sawing logs, with a two-handed saw as big as himself, in what he (Balaam) considered a most inefficient manner. Balaam's passion to instruct was so keen and the old man's courtesy was so charming that my friend did not notice, until he had finished, that he had been sawing up all the timber in Portgower. I suspect that canny, white-bearded old Highlander, for all his charming manner, of having a mischievous eye. I have not been unguilty of the same attitude at home, when visitors from town have despised my method of handling a lawn mower, and my urban friends have paid (as, I suspect, Balaam paid) for their scorn in hard labour.

Not that Balaam minded in the least. There is a childish but by no means despicable pleasure in stout physical effort, and by the time that Portgower's logs were sawn, Balaam was so pleased with himself and the whole world, that he ended his feat by distributing pennies among the entire juvenile population of Portgower, which had turned out, to a baby, to do him the honour of watching his exploit. Furthermore, the effort had made him disgracefully hungry again. There is a little room in Portgower (where we consumed an almost indecent quantity of boiled eggs, hot scones and black-currant jelly) which is like no room I have seen anywhere else. That room is the epitome of an age, which did not seem picturesque when it was in being—what age ever does ?—but now has a halo of rather wistful romance. An untouched, unspoiled Victorian parlour, a perfect period piece. It contains a marble mantelpiece, an exotic bunch of wax-fruit under a glass-dome, a mechanical rocking-chair with metal springs, a round mahogany table with feet like a dragon's, a piano with a pleated green silk shirt-front and two large lithographed portraits, one of Mr. Gladstone and the other of Dr. Norman Macleod, D.D. If a dramatist wished to write a period play—something with real old-world charm—he could not have a better " set " than this perfect parlour at Portgower. (Incidentally, he could not find better scones, except, perhaps, at Sandhaven, but that is neither here nor there.) We were also delighted with two faded but delicious period photographs, showing civic celebrations at Golspie and Brora on the occasion of a visit to Dunrobin by the Prince of Wales and his charming bride, the young Princess Alexandra. There was something awe-inspiring in the picture of the bearded village worthies, picturesquely grouped in their loyal lum hats, under a

triumphal arch, which bore the legend, FLOREAT
BRORA. And when I think of the beautiful princess
and those lum hats that came out to do her honour,
I will maintain to my dying day my old contention
that the Victorian Age was an age of pure romance.

The road dips down into Helmsdale before it
rises sharply again, and by the bridge where the
river runs out to sea, I stopped to take two photographs: one of the ruined castle at the river mouth
where an earl of Sutherland and his countess were
done to death by poison, through the machinations
of the wicked Earl of Caithness; another of a group
of ragged, brown-skinned tinker-children, who,
seeing a camera, came and posed for their photographs with all the aplomb of artists' models.
There is a picturesque inevitability about the tinker
caravanserai—the same ramshackle cart, piled with
kettles, clothes-pegs and babies, the same shaggy,
sturdy pony, the same covey of healthy, dirty
children. The sight of bright-eyed tinker-children
always makes me wonder whether "clean dirt" is as
harmful to the young as modern hygiene would
have us believe. But, sentimentalist though I
may be, I am still disinclined to believe that dirt
is a virtue in itself. I merely think that wind and
sun are splendidly able to render it comparatively
harmless. Still, I only wish that the sedate and
well-scrubbed children of my own village looked as
lively and healthy as those tinker-urchins on the
bridge at Helmsdale.

Higher up the village we came upon a sight as romantic as anything that ever came out of the Middle Ages—the authentic troubadour, or itinerant entertainer, of 1932. But he was no mere wandering minstrel, with lute and repertory of ballads. Outside the village hall, he was descending from a huge lorry, flamboyantly labelled: TALKIES on TOUR.

In this large house on wheels he kept, not merely his projector, sound apparatus and screen, but his wife and family.

"I used to do this job, stopping at lodgings in every town I was showing," he told us, "but you'd have thought I was Andrew Carnegie, the prices they charged. But I fixed them. I've got the old lorry as cosy as a Kelvinside villa. Now I can snap my fingers at the old landladies. There's comfort in your own house, even if you're driving up and down the roads, and nobody knows that better than me that's lived half my life with a circus."

He talked to us of his work, and spoke rather cynically, as is the way of all public entertainers when they discuss their profession.

"It's a fair knock-out to tell what they want," he said, they being that exasperating, enigmatical body, the great British public. "*You* don't know what they want. I don't know. Half the time, they don't know themselves. At least it isn't so much a question of not knowing what they want, as not knowing *how* they want it. You never can tell. Sometimes, you can get away with a dud, and other times you can show a sure-fire winner and go down on your knees to them, but will they come in? They stop outside, smokin' their fags, and waitin' for their pals to come in. What with that, and wondering whether the Talkie's goin' to talk or not, and waitin' for them to cry out for their money back, it's a bit of a job. I'm the only man that's ever shown Talkies on the Isle of Skye, and they waited till midnight because the sound-jigger went wrong and had to be sorted. Still, they went home happy, even if it was the first time in their lives they'd been out of their beds after nine o'clock."

I sympathised with him on the well-known vagaries in public taste, from which no one suffers more than the working novelist.

"I don't know," he replied philosophically. "That's the thanks you get for educatin' the public taste. The more you educate them, the higher they turn up their noses. I've known the time when these folk would have walked miles to see dissolvin' views of the minister's trip to Palestine, but will they now? *Will they just?* I know them. They're that pernickety, they expect a free sample before they come in. But whatever they want and whatever they don't want, there's always two things that'll go down. Those two things ll get you anywhere, if you mix them the right way. They want Love—just enough of it, and not too much of the close-up cuddlin'—and they want Fightin'. Love and Fightin'—that's the stuff they can never have too much of, but you've got to convince them that's what they're goin' to get, or you might as well use your screen for a bed-sheet. Look at that," he said, pointing to a poster pasted to the side of the lorry. "There's a daft title for you. If it hasn't got Love or Fightin' in it, it's no good. I could give them tips on titles"—he indicated all Hollywood with a scornful gesture—"but you know what it is. They'll never listen to a practical man. Still, it's a way of makin' a livin', and if it wasn't for the sciatica and the Entertainment Tax, I'd not grumble. It's better than workin' in a circus, any way. Mind you, I don't get sciatica from livin' in a lorry, it's drivin' the old brute at five miles an hour, with your leg stuck in one position that does it."

We wished him good luck and a good house, with confusion to the sciatica and the collectors of Entertainment Tax. Then we slowly climbed on to the high ridge that is called the Ord of Caithness. This is a wild, bold mountain road, skirting great gorges on a narrow shelf with bare moorland above and rocky cliffs, falling sheer to the sea, below. Fine as the road has been, it is still being improved and extensive operations are going on to make it the finest hill-road in Britain. While the road is up, however, passage is not altogether pleasant, and Balaam, obliged to slow down to a snail's pace,

cursed the road and its makers with hearty curses.
It was along this road that an incident occurred to
Mr. Balaam which proves that history repeats itself,
for it was almost identical in point with the episode
of Dr. Johnson and the waiter at the "sorry inn"
of Montrose. We were held up while a cart dis-
charged its cargo of stones on the road, and, as we
waited, Balaam took the opportunity of expressing
his views on Scottish roads and their makers to the
foreman in charge of the gang. My friend rose
to great heights of invective, explaining how much
more intelligently they did these things in England,
and pointing out, in an eloquent peroration, how
only an imbecile or a Scotsman would have incon-
venienced us in that way. The little foreman never
moved a muscle while the flood of vituperation
poured over him, but when the torrent had ceased,
he took his cutty pipe from his mouth, and, still
without a word, pointed with it at the roadside lorry
on which were inscribed the words:

JOHN SMITH
CONTRACTOR
LONDON.

(I have not set down the correct name of the
firm, but it was as unmistakably English as that.)

Balaam did not speak for a long time after we had
passed the lorry. "Anyway," he said at last, "it'll
be a magnificent piece of road engineering . . .
when it's finished."

Still climbing steeply, we reached the top of the hill that looks down over Berriedale, and from there the road sweeps down with a vengeance. At this point we stopped. We were in Caithness, wildest and barest of Scotland's counties. At many a point on this road you can stand and see nothing at all, except the sea on the one hand, and a rolling expanse of bare heather bents on the other. A lovely sight in summer, maybe, but a place of dark desolation at any other time of the year. Near the top of the hill there is a kindly notice which advises nervous cyclists to take the emergency road at the side, but we discovered, on investigation, that this was not a road at all; only a little by-lane into which you might suddenly turn for safety if you found yourself running away. Looking from the other side of the road, we gazed down into a wild, wooded gorge, where water foamed and the trees climbed steeply. At the bottom of the hill there is a narrow bridge and a devil's elbow of a turn before the road suddenly shoots upwards again. Overlooking the farther corner of the bend is a house whose entire front is decorated with stags' antlers. At Berriedale two rivers flow into the sea and the village lies at their mouth, but what with the bend and the bridge and the sudden sight of the stags' antlers—on which he fears he may be impaled if he does not judge the "elbow" to a nicety—the motorist is apt to miss the beauties of this prettily placed village. So I suggest to the traveller that he leaves his car in the thoughtfully provided emergency road and walks down the road, to see the glen—which is a miniature Affric—the village and the ruined castle, which belonged to the turbulent Sinclairs, earls of Caithness.

Our climb northward out of Berriedale was the steepest—indeed the only genuinely steep climb—of our journey, if you except our vague wanderings in the neighbourhood of Pennan, which were probably due to our own fault, but so well did the little car behave that when we breasted the top of the rise, Balaam expressed a desire to get out and pat her bonnet. The country looking inland from the sea is a trackless expanse of deer-forest. The word "forest," I need hardly say, is merely a technical term, for what you see is a vast treeless waste of bare bleak moorland with tufts of brown dead heather covering the dark peaty soil. We left the car and climbed a steep bank above the road to see further expanses of brown heather moor, stretching out endlessly. Suddenly on the next ridge appeared a pair of antlers and then a big stag loomed up on the sky-line, followed by the rest of the herd. That old Solomon of a stag, with his wives, came gliding across our field of view, without appearing to be in the least alarmed by our presence. No doubt they knew it was not the stalking-season or, in any case, were convinced that we meant them no harm. So they passed in solemn file and disappeared over the ridge again, having, as Balaam said, "done their stuff" for us very nicely. They seemed much tamer than the deer in Glen Affric, which shot down like lightning into a deep corrie at the first sound of our approach.

"If I'd brought one of those old deer-stalker caps that you see in the old Sherlock Holmes illustrations," said Balaam, "they wouldn't have treated us so lightly."

The view on the seaward side was magnificent. Though we might have thought from the map that we were nearing the end of our journey, the coast still stretched out northward before us in a seemingly endless panorama of high rocky promontories, cold, stark and grey. The end of the road was not to come for a long while yet. We passed along a bleak road where the only signs of habitation were little low thinly-thatched cabins. How meagre and starved-looking is this Caithness thatch, compared with the thick, golden, opulent-looking thatch of an Essex village, which gives the cottages an air of well-being and content. Here there is every evidence of a continuous struggle against cold, wind and rain, as though the very houses themselves were hard put to it. Before coming down to Dunbeath, where we saw brightly painted fishing-boats by the shore, we saw Dunbeath Castle, which was captured by Montrose in one of his swift northern raids. At Dunbeach, on the narrow bridge, we saw a shepherd's dog carrying home the morning paper in its mouth, and the sight of a morning paper in these parts reminded us that evening was coming on. For some reason or other, Balaam was suddenly smitten with a wild desire to camp out. Why he should have chosen the wilder parts of Caithness for this strange fancy, when we might have camped at any one of a dozen milder spots farther south, I cannot say. His mind was made up. The tent was in the back of the car. What was the sense, he argued, of carrying a perfectly good tent right to John o' Groats, if you did not sleep in it even once? So, at Latheron, where there is a strange old upright stone-slab, which goes back to pre-Norse and even pre-Celtic times, we turned off the coast-road to seek shelter for the night. This road cuts across-country to Thurso, and passes over long stretches of desolate moorland.

We stopped at a little croft and asked permission to camp for the night nearby. The crofter, a bent little old man, who looked as if he had been standing up against a hard, biting wind all his life, courteously indicated the moorland in front, which looked as if it might embrace at least the half of Caithness, and told us we were welcome. He seemed pleased to talk to strangers, and was what we call "well-spoken" and even well-read, though I admit it is merely snobbish to be surprised that a peasant should read good books. It was something of a shock to meet close at hand a method of life which, considered in political and social theory, has always attracted me. Here, in the flesh, was the ideal

Chestertonian peasant, living on what he produced, and untouched by the modern evils of industrial and urban civilisation. If capitalism is a curse, it did not hurt him, and socialism, whether as curse or a blessing, could not affect him in any way. He has his bit of land, and as long as he works desperately hard he can keep himself in food, fuel and shelter.

Is it a good life? The worst of testing our theories by the facts is not so much that it makes us fling our theories away, which would be something definite, but that it makes us feel more doubtful and puzzled than we were before. If complexity is the supreme evil of modern life, then the crofter is better off than we are. His life is truly simple—a simple battle for food and warmth. He has none of the worries of factory smoke, of noise, of meaningless hustle and rush. He has secure tenure of his land, a cow, a sheep or two and a few hens, all of which may reasonably induce a nobler pride of ownership than the townsman's part-paid-for car, gramophone or wireless-set. His kitchen is cosy, with its peat fire, and he at least is his own man there.

But . . . it is a cold, cold place, where the biting wind skirls ceaselessly over the moor. The land is bare and starved and sour. The sheep have a lean and hungry look. Even the kail in the kitchen garden has a windswept stunted appearance. Everything speaks of a strenuous daily struggle for bare existence. While I will do my crofter the justice to say that he seemed contented with his lot, I am more at sea than ever with my theory of the happy peasant. It may be a good life, but I am convinced that, for all the ideal theories of freedom and peasant-proprietorship, it is not *the* good life. It is too hard, too cold, too bleak. . . .

We drove the car, somewhat gingerly, over a stone track, which led on to the moor, where nothing grew but the rough, tufty cotton grass—cannich, the Caithness people call it. The sheep will nibble the cannich when it is young, but it seems a meagre substitute for sweet green grass. On the edge of the moor we attempted to set up our tent. I have often written (and sometimes even read) articles in comic papers about people who put up tents in lonely places and have their guy-ropes chewed by goats and their centre-pole removed by inquisitive cows. Things do not happen in real life as they happen in comic papers. On the edge of that Caithness moor, anything so friendly and companionable as a cow would have been welcome, but the crofter's cow, safe in its rough stone byre, had more intelligence than we had. The wind did not blow in sharp gusts, but in one long "bitter, blaudin'" blast that pierced to the marrow and took the breath from the lungs. The tent-canvas stood out horizontally, not flapping irritably, as in ordinary winds, but simply resisting all efforts to tug it into a vertical position. Balaam and I indulged in a shouting match at less than a yard's distance, but no intelligible communication passed between us. Our words were simply hurled across the moor on the wings of the wind. At last I saw Balaam gesticulating wildly, and though I could not hear a single word, I managed to gather that he was pointing in the direction of a rough circular stone wall which lay farther over on the right. Our feet stumbled forward, the tent canvas bellied out like a sail, and we found ourselves being hurled along over squelching peat-bog and innumerable tiny burns, until we staggered, breathless, under the lee of the stone wall. We had found one of those circular pounds where the sheep are driven for shelter in winter. To be out of that wind was like reaching haven after a wild storm. Inside the pound, our tent allowed itself to be erected, snug and trim, and, after a supper of boiled eggs which we had obtained from the crofter's wife, we slept in reasonable warmth and comfort. But, had it not been for the shelter of the sheep-pound, I think we should have perished.

In the morning we bade good-bye to the crofter and told him that, while we liked his countryside, we found the wind rather cold.

"Yess," he replied politely, "it iss being cold, *but not so cold as it wass being last Chune.*"

photographers. They are doing their own work on their own ground and no one could do it with more efficiency or less ostentation.

Wick, for its size, is a place of narrow twisted streets, and it is possible, if you do not know your way, to wander into all sorts of dead-ends and queer back alleys, finding the quay and losing it again, before you strike the right northward route.

About three miles north of Wick, the road strikes sharply to the right and swings towards the wide sweep of Sinclair's Bay. There are low links on the right, and the road, which has hitherto been surprisingly good, grows rougher and stonier. Signs of successful cultivation become fewer. At Keiss, a largish village, we saw a ruined castle and—a rather more imposing sight—a giant cement-mixer hard at work upon materials for road-improvement. Not a tree could be seen anywhere. The red sandstone road wound uncertainly over dark moorland, where the holes from which the peat had been dug showed blacker than the peat itself.

We left the car and walked across the edge of the moorland to watch a crofter and his two daughters cutting peat. He was standing against a bare ridge (as it might have been a coal "face") and using a curious long-handled implement that seemed to be half a stilt and half a spade. Thus, by pressing downward, he was able to cut two surfaces at once, cleanly slicing off the peat in blocks about a foot square and three inches thick.

As he cut each peat his daughter seized it and flung it deftly up on to the bank behind, where her younger sister caught it and added it to her rapidly growing pile.

The crofter told us that he was laying in his stock of winter firing. Just as every little chalet in Switzerland has its stock of sawn pine-logs, so every Caithness croft has its peat-stack. He told us that these peats would take a fortnight to dry. (They were very wet now and the firm, white forearm of the girl who was flinging them on to the bank was stained an oozy black almost to the elbow.) When they were dry, they would be carted to the stack beside the croft and then, after they had been stacked for another fortnight, they would be ready for use.

"There's some that don't like the reek of a peat-fire," the old man said, "but I like it fine myself. And mind you, we're needing good fires up here in the winter-time, with the winds that are blowing along the Pentland."

Winter, as we stood there, was a thought to make a Southerner shiver, for even then the wind blew shrilly over the peat-moss, and the girls, though they were doing warm, muscular work, wore heavy skirts and thick woollen jerseys.

"Yes," said the old man, "winter's a sore time and we have to be making the most of the summer, and now even the summer's not the good time it was years ago. In the old days a few crofters—

For the rest, the views of the most northerly boy may be put down, after the usual fashion of the interviewer, in one sentence.

"Master ——, who maintained that Duncansby Head, though a cold place, was much like other places, expressed himself as contented with life in general, but viewed with repugnance the growing habit, on the part of cigarette-manufacturers, of substituting coupons for pictures, his opinion of coupons, considered as works of art or a medium of exchange, being exceedingly low."

We parted rather sadly from this little boy, because, although he was a gentleman and did not upbraid us, we knew he must feel that we had let him down in this important matter of cigarette cards, nor was it much use explaining that the fault lay with the said manufacturers rather than with ourselves. So we came down the winding cliff road again to look for John o' Groat's House.

This house, like so many of the things we believe in and talk of every day, does not exist, though it is easy to find the spot, near the hotel on the low shore, where it once stood. The legend of John o' Groats varies considerably, and you are at liberty to pick out those parts of the story which attract you most. All the stories agree that there was a John o' Groats and that he had an eight-sided house. The excellent hotel has an eight-sided gable, so that at least is a piece of honest octagonal evidence. One story holds that he was a ferry-man who charged you a groat for rowing you over to the Isle of Stroma and that his house had a little shelter on each of its eight sides, so that you would be protected from the wind, whichever way it blew.

"No," said Balaam, "I won't have that. In the first place, would any Scotsman undertake so hazardous a journey for fourpence?"

"Why not? Fourpence was worth a good deal more than fourpence in those very pre-War days. Besides, the best authorities maintain that he was not a Scotsman, but a Dutchman, named Johan de Groot."

"In any case," said Balaam, "I won't accept your eight-sided ferry-shelter. From my small experience of this coast, I would say that the wind blows from a hundred directions and not merely eight. Objection sustained?"

I fear this objection must be sustained. The other story is that Johan de Groot had seven brothers —or possibly eight sons—who were always quarrelling for precedence, and so he built his eight-sided house round an eight-sided table so that each person could walk in, slam his own door and sit down at the head of the board.

" A cantankerous family," said Balaam. "Eight doors and a prevailing wind like this. All I can say is, it must have been a dashed draughty house. Living in it must have been one continuous grand slam."

We walked to the end of the concrete jetty which

ran out to the water along a beach of broken, brightly coloured shells. The seas beat at our feet with a heavy, threatening roar, as though they resented even this mild attempt to reach a point a little farther north. The Isle of Stroma rose out of the grey water before us, but beyond, though we strained our eyes, we caught no glimpse of the promised cliffs of Hoy. A heavy grey haze lay on the water. The Pentland Firth looked threatening and hostile, and I thought that John o' Groats (or Groot) with his fourpenny ferry-boat, must have been a very bold fellow. From the faint outline that sometimes appeared, only to be lost in the mist, the Orkneys seemed no pleasant fabled Orcades, but grey and rocky isles, set in turbulent seas, that would resent intrusion. We were to see them under a serener sky, but now, seen at odd moments across the troubled waters, they lowered at us in most unfriendly fashion. Standing on the jetty, Balaam told me a story of an uncle of his, a clergyman of mild and inoffensive character, who once took a holiday trip to the Orkneys and never came back.

" No," said Balaam, "he was not drowned in the Pentland Firth. It was sadder than that. He was so deathly sea-sick on the voyage that when he landed at Kirkwall, he swore a mighty oath that nothing—not even the offer of two bishoprics— would induce him to set foot on a steamer-deck again. So he changed his denomination, undertook a cure

JOHN O' GROATS

"The end of all things . . ."

Photo by Valentine & Sons, Ltd.

of souls, and lived in the Orkneys, respected by all who knew him, for nineteen years. And when people wrote and asked him why he had become a Presbyterian, he replied that he would become a Mohammedan rather than endure a Pentland Firth sea-sickness again. A very sad case."

I have spoken in friendly fashion of the most northerly boy in Britain, but I had not hitherto considered him in bulk. As we returned from the jetty, a horde of him bore down on us, waving in our faces picture-postcards and necklaces made from the sea-shells of John o' Groats. So fierce was the onset, so menacing was the mob, that Balaam was obliged to force it back with hands outstretched. Then, holding off the crowd of urchins at arm's length, he proceeded to address to them a stern harangue, upon the decay of modern manners, the evils of unrestricted competition, the commercial depravity of demanding twopence for a penny postcard, and, above all, the extreme rudeness of pushing a prospective customer. Then, with extreme dignity, he walked over to a solitary, under-sized laddie who had not taken part in the scrimmage, and purchased from him two necklaces and a dozen postcards.

"There," said Balaam, grandiloquently pointing the moral. "No wonder your ancestors needed an eight-sided house. My money goes to the boy who didn't push. Let that be a lesson to you all."

For a moment the ranks of Tuscany gazed on

him dumbly. They were dazed by his eloquence. Then from somewhere among that little crowd came the retort, loud and unmistakable: "Sez you!"

Let me repeat that. By John o' Groats, at the uttermost edge of Britain's farthest boundary, where sea-birds moan and the waves beat sullenly——there, at the end of all things, a perky small boy shouted at Mr. Balaam: "*Sez you!*"

*　　*　　*　　*　　*

"And that," said Balaam as we drove away, "is the original universal language your poor King James was so anxious to discover."

It was of no use for me to argue that the misguided lad must have learnt the objectionable expression while visiting, say, on a rare birthday-treat, some picture palace at Wick. Balaam would have none of it. All the way to Thurso he kept muttering: "The universal language. And *what* a language!"

XVII

RETREAT FROM TONGUE

UNDER lowering grey skies we drove along the twisting road towards Thurso, over country where the peaty soil was as black as coal-dust. There were no hedges and no stone walls, but every little field seemed to be surrounded by a line of grave-stones. I don't know if these thin slabby stones, of which all the hedges are made, are the Caithness flags which are sent out from Thurso to furnish paving-stones for the world's great cities. I only know they give the countryside an eerie look, when you pass along endless lanes of them under a low and leaden sky. We discovered that these flag-hedges were not really gravestones, when we found the little grey kirkyard, just beyond Huna, which belongs to the most northerly church in Scotland; a lonely spot for a last resting-place containing, alas, many a sailor's grave.

The road rises towards Mey, and under the lee of the slope we saw a little belt of trees—the first trees we had seen for a long while, but while nature might be somewhat milder inland, the coast was still wild, barren and rocky. A little later we passed the Loch of St. John, a lonely stretch of water that lies between the road and the sea. There were houses beyond, and soon we came to the village of Dunnet, whence a road which is not much better than a cart-track goes out to that wild headland, which is the authentic northernmost point of Britain's mainland. We saw the promontory at a distance, a huge, lumpy mass, surmounted by a pencil of lighthouse, beyond which sky and sea met in one long band of sullen grey.

Though Dunnet Head is as wild and lonely a crag as eagle could choose for a nest, its defiant strength gives shelter and comfort to the little golden bay that lies beyond. It is a long way to come, but the sight of that tranquil bay is worth an arduous journey. As we came out by the low sand-hills the sky cleared and the sun shone down on one of the brightest stretches of golden sand we had seen in the whole of our travels. You could plant here a wonderful seaside resort if it were not so far from anywhere. . . .

We continued our way along a "linky" shore where undulating sandy dunes rose and fell between us and the sea. Here, for the moment, was no longer a country of barren crofts, for we saw several fair-sized farms, with "gravestone" hedges round their fields and, in the stackyard of one of them, a tall tower which was no ancient keep, but a modern silo.

Castletown has no castle, so far as we could see, but—strange sight in the northern hinterland—it has a factory, where our gravestone "flags" are cut and shaped. Near Castleton, we saw a little patch of woodland, which came as another surprise, for we had not thought to see a really good clump of

trees again until we turned far south. Johnson
swore that there were only two trees in Fife and
that the thorn which Mary Queen of Scots planted
at St. Andrews was the only piece of timber in
Scotland older than himself. A foolish statement
to make about Fife, but one that might be maintained
with better show of probability in Caithness. How
he would have laughed to see this little oasis near
Castletown!

Before you enter Thurso, by crossing the river
of the same name, you come suddenly at a sweeping
bend, upon Thurso Castle, a turreted, baronial pile,
rebuilt upon the site of an ancient Sinclair stronghold which went back to the times when the earls
of Caithness were also earls of Orkney. There have
always been famous Sinclairs. The earlier bearers
of that name were doughty warriors; one built a
castle at Kirkwall so strong that his enemies said
the Evil One helped him to lay the stones; another
marched south to die for his king at Flodden and a
third was slain, striving to regain his heritage of the
Orkneys, but, in many ways, the most attractive of
them all would seem to be that Sir John Sinclair
who was no warrior, but a great farmer-statesman
—a much greater figure than most of the gilded
names which adorned eighteenth-century cabinets.
He was one of the few who had the courage to dis-
agree with Pitt, and showed even greater courage
and resource in his efforts to improve local and
national agriculture. After all, it may be a fine

ideal to set out with the hope of making two blades of grass grow where one grew before, but the man who could begin the fulfilment of that ideal in bare and boggy Caithness must have been something of a hero. He was the first, and possibly the best president of the Board of Agriculture, and he wrote a sort of contemporary Doomsday book—a Statistical Account of Scotland, which gave a survey of every parish in the country and still remains a mine of interest and information. He was born at the castle and his statue, by Chantrey, stands near the church.

Thurso was once the great seaport for trade with the early Norsemen. Its very name is Norse, for the river on whose mouth it was built was called Thor's river. In the Middle Ages it was a thriving port, and now, unlike so many ports from whom the tide of sea-going commerce has flowed away, it has not allowed itself to fall into decay, but still remains the market-centre of the agriculture which good Sir John Sinclair helped to its feet and also of the industry which produces the Caithness flags.

In the harbour town, which is delightfully named Fisher-biggins, there is a ruined church which is older than any in Caithness. We are apt to think of the Norsemen only as sea-raiders and pirates, but Thurso's history tells of long periods of peaceful trading, during which Thurso merchants grew richer and more powerful than any in the north.

After Thurso's wide main street, the road climbs steeply from the town. It also turns slightly inland so that we did not go down to the little port of Scrabster, whence the mailboat crosses to the Orkneys; but after the sinister story of Balaam's clerical uncle, I was slightly nervous of the sight of even an Orkney mailboat. Gradually descending the westward slope of Scrabster Hill to cross the bridge over the River Forss, we caught a glimpse of shimmering sea under a clear sky. Evening was coming on now, but the clouds which had followed from John o' Groats and Dunnet Head had cleared away, leaving a sea of dancing silver where the slanting sunlight fell from over the shoulders of the cliffs and headlands that lay before us. Under a dark sky, all the northern coast is hostile and unfriendly, but when the storm-clouds roll back and the westering sunbeams touch the water, there you have a sea that might wash the shores of fairy-land.

After we had passed Reay, which was once a stronghold of the clan Mackay, we came out upon high bare moorland where the country was the wildest of the wild. Before and behind the eye could follow the ribbon of road till it was lost in a fold of the moor. On either side we could see nothing but a rolling expanse of dead heather-bents. Balaam stopped his engine. There was an eerie silence, broken only by the faint rustle of a burn among the dead heather. Not a tree—not a

271

bird—was in sight. It was a loneliness of desolation; a loneliness that pressed like a weight upon
your head.

"If you were stranded here," said Balaam lugu-
briously, "you wouldn't have a friendly crow to
pick your bones. Or, supposing, you were taken
ill, you wouldn't have a . . ."

On our ears broke the sound of a motor-engine
and soon there slipped by us a very small car in
which sat, not a reiver or motor-bandit, but a
district nurse.

Civilisation is a cheerful and heartening thing.
It may have its drawbacks, but, when, in the uttermost wilds, a man has only to talk about being ill to
produce a qualified nurse, then, civilisation may be
said to be worth while.

We crossed the River Halladale by a fine bridge of
stone and steel; after that we followed a road that
ran round a little rocky bay and then climbed above
it. At the top of the hill we stopped to chat with
a young man whose well-cut clothes suggested that
he was a southerner, but whose voice, entirely
devoid as it was of accent, gave us no clue to
his "native parts." Evening was falling quickly
and rather chill, and we were ready to put up for
the night. Our struggle of the previous night
with wind and tent-ropes, however, had suggested
that one night's camping in Caithness was quite
enough.

"There's a very good hotel just up the road,"

the young man said, "but if you don't want to go
there——"

"We don't," said Balaam, "we're feeling much too
disreputable for good hotels."

"Well," said the young man, with a pleasant
twinkle, "my father has just started a small road-
house, and I think you'd be comfortable there.   If
you'd like to garage your car in the byre, we can just
push the old cow over a bit."

There was plenty of room for the car in the byre
without seriously incommoding the cow, and we
sat down to supper in the "road-house," well content with the world.   Although it was a wooden
building it was no rough shanty.   It had been built
by local carpenters, who were evidently proud
craftsman, for every join in the wooden walls showed
beautiful workmanship.   The boards had a faint,
pleasant woody smell, which mingling with the
delectable scent of frying bacon gave a friendly
invitation to supper.

After the meal, we strolled up the village with
our young acquaintance in the soft evening light
and looked down on the sea which was now so still,
giving no hint of the storms and dangers of wild
weather.   He told us old stories of storms and
wreckage; of one of Nelson's ships that was on her
way to the breakers' yard but was driven on to the
cruel rocks below and never concluded her last
journey.   He told us, too, of a wild night of tempest
long ago, when the superstitious fisherfolk of

Portskerra, the village at the mouth of the bay, lay shivering and praying in their beds. The foul fiend was abroad on the wings of the storm, and well they knew it, for did they not hear his deathly shrieks resounding through the night? When the pale dawn broke, the Portskerra folk crept down to the shore and there they found that an emigrant ship had been smashed to pieces on the rocks. There were masses of floating wreckage and many a body that must be laid in a nameless grave in Portskerra kirkyard.

Other stories he told us that had been handed down in the family; of the cruel evictions of a hundred years ago, when the Highlanders had been driven out from their beautiful Strath Naver and forced to settle on little crofts by the shore.

"They might have got a good bit of land or a bad one. They were just dumped down. Even if a family has been settled for a hundred years, it knows that Strath Naver is its real home."

After the chill of the evening had driven us indoors we sat and yarned over the glow of a peat fire. He told us something of the story of his father's life, which would have made a novel in itself. When his father was a little boy, he was left an orphan in the care of a widowed mother, but this redoubtable old lady was no pathetic widow of fiction.

"She was six feet high and as strong as a grenadier. There wasn't a man in the countryside that wasn't afraid of her. When, as a lad, he went courting my mother, the old woman wouldn't hear of it. She gave him such black looks that, as soon as he could get my mother to promise to wait for him, he cleared out to America to make his fortune. He was a blacksmith by trade and had the shoeing of all the horses that came along the road to Tongue, in the days before motor-cars. He did well in America, and when he had made enough money to be independent, he came back and married my mother, who'd been waiting for him all the time. Now my brothers and I are all decently started in life—I'm in the hotel business myself—but the old man could not settle down to be idle, so he started this road-house for the sake of something to do. He'll look after his visitors very well, though I wouldn't say they mightn't be neglected, if a horse came along that needed shoeing. He still thinks a blacksmith's is the only life for a real man."

We drank a glass of milk from the garage-cow, and then slept soundly in a little room with a pleasant woody smell, where we did not waken till the morning sun came streaming in through our windows.

We started early and were granted a sight for the gods: morning sun over a sea of pearl and silver and a glimpse of the Orkneys, not as a hostile and forbidding land, but as isles of faëry. As the sunlight glinted on the dimpling waters the story of Balaam's uncle dropped, lost and forgotten, to the bottom of Melvich Bay. There, under a cloudless sky, were the fabled Orcades, summer isles, for an enchanting moment, in a summer sea.

The sunlight was welcome. We needed all that could be given us, for our way lay over open moorland, almost unimaginably bare. The only speck of colour against that of the moss was the white of the sheep, that wandered, at will, on moor and roadway, with their new-born children. We watched what the poet calls "the frisky frolic of the little lanky lambs." Their favourite frolic seemed to be the game, well known to London children, which is called "Last Across the Road." They would wait until Balaam slowed down and then indulged in what he described as community-jumping right in front of our bonnet. We crossed the Strathy Water near to where it flows into the sea and caught sight of a pretty little beach that looked bright and golden in the sunlight. The coast is broken and storm-beaten, and every sign speaks of wild seas and rough weather, but while the sunshine of a spring morning which is better than "the essential silence," cheers and blesses, storms may be forgotten. Moorland again, a few signs of human life and habitation: a tinker encampment with children crawling in the doorways of ragged tents and Shetland ponies tethered nearby; a lonely shepherd, calling his dog to heel and scanning the horizon with field-glasses; and then, a strange sight but sure evidence of civilisation, a letter-box nailed to a pole. Then, on another stretch of the wildest moorland, we came upon great clumps of wild irises. They grew under the lee of a slope that protected them from the north wind and their hue was a vivid purple. Those irises would have been beautiful anywhere, but on the dun, bare moorland they were the bravest of brave sights. After we passed them, the desolation was complete. Nothing but rough moss flanked the road, and high bare slopes, with snow in the corries, loomed far ahead. At Bettyhill we were not sure of our way, but a friendly dominie came out from his school playground and showed us where the road bent back sharply to the left. It was at Bettyhill that we saw the last of those little golden bays of the north, that stick so closely in the memory. You may forget the cold winds and the jagged cliffs and the peaty moss, but you will always remember the little golden beaches which, under their rare sunlight, are of the stuff of dreams.

The road on which the dominie set us winds for a mile or two along the banks of the pretty River Naver, which flows down from the lovely green strath, whence the crofters were driven out a hundred years ago. It is a clear and limpid stream and, where the sunlight touched it, the sand on its bed gleamed golden. We crossed the Naver by a good bridge, and then wandered southward along its pleasant western bank until we struck the main road for Tongue, which again brought us out on to bare moorland, with the same mountain-masses towering ahead. It had been a radiant morning when we had set out, but now clouds were scurrying across the sky, like war-clans gathering in the west. The mountains were black where the thickening clouds rode above them, but covered with streaks and patches of gold where the sun still peeped through. We crossed Borgie Bridge, where the local 'bus politely waited for us to pass, and drove along towards the shores of the Kyle of Tongue. The moorland was less wild and we saw little belts of trees, but they were bent, gnarled and windswept. In just the same way the few old cottage-people whom we met along the road, seemed gnarled and bent, too! As the road reaches the shores of the Kyle, it turns southwards towards the village of Tongue, leaving a last glimpse of little islands in the opening of the firth. The clouds were still thickening and there was only one small patch of blue sky through which the sunlight still peeped. Sadly we watched the gap close. Sky and sea were grey.

It was raining hard when we drove into Tongue; raining when we looked at the massive walls of ruined Castle Varrich; raining when we drew up for petrol at the hotel-garage by the shore. There were heavy clouds on the tremendous shoulders of Ben Loyal and Ben Hope. We had seen snow on Ben Hope earlier in the morning, but now the rainclouds were blotting the mountains out.

When the garage-hand cheerfully opined that it was fine weather for the fishing, Balaam shrugged his shoulders.

"Will it rain all day?" he asked.

"I've known it rain for a week with the wind in this quarter," said the optimist. (He really *was* an optimist, because the people who come to Tongue for fishing have views upon the weather different from those of other mortals.)

The rain came down, not in a swift shower, but steadily, relentlessly, inexorably. We waited for an hour, but the rain, it seemed, was prepared, like a relentless poker player, to face us out.

"I'm afraid," said Balaam reluctantly, "that that's that."

"I'm afraid it is."

"I dislike your country sufficiently not to want to be beaten by it, but I have a superstitious dislike of being drowned by rain. Between us and Cape Wrath there are twenty miles of not-too-good road, and then another dozen miles, if I mistake not, of footslogging. Now to attempt that in this weather, I contend, would be unlucky. I really think we might take Cape Wrath as read."

So Tongue was, if not our Waterloo, at least our Moscow, for from Tongue we retreated in ignominy (and drenching rain) having failed to pursue the coast to its north-western corner, where the lighthouse of Cape Wrath flings out its mighty beam. Instead of pursuing the tortuous way

279

westward along the western shores of Tongue and across dark moorland to skirt peaceful Loch Eriboll, we turned tail towards Altnaharra and Lairg, to Bonar Bridge and over the Struie to Dingwall, and so southward and homeward. . . .

"Well," said Balaam, as we splashed along the road that follows the bare shore of long, narrow Loch Loyal, "are you satisfied this time?"

"Amply satisfied, except that we didn't reach Cape Wrath or even Durness. In some ways this was the most interesting of our three journeys. We may not have come on anything so grand as Glen Affric, but we've seen a whole heap of lovely things: the evening view of Auld Reekie from Burntisland with the Castle Rock floating in cloud, the bright boats in the haven at St. Monans, Strathmore from the cemetery above Kirriemuir, the cottage gardens at Rosemarkie, the sight of the Orkneys in pearly sunlight, and all the little golden bays of far north."

"Not forgetting," added Balaam, "the noble high tea at Sandhaven, the lady of the whales at Bonar Bridge, and the young universal linguist who said 'Sez you' at John o' Groats."

*   *   *   *   *

When I last saw Balaam he was in his garden and I do not think he need have answered "Winter broccoli" quite so truculently when I asked him what he was planting. Is it likely that anyone would send him a parcel containing winter broccoli

—a parcel, mark you, which was posted not a hundred miles from the spot where my woman-hating friend had once looked down upon the high-road over the North Sea and magically conjured up a little sugar for his tea? Winter broccoli? I think not. I may be no botanist, but at least I know the difference between winter broccoli and something which is, in my opinion, much more charming.

And if ever I wished to write a thrilling detective story (not without feminine interest) I might head my first chapter:

Mr. Balaam and the Mystery of the White Heather.

THE END.

INDEX

INDEX

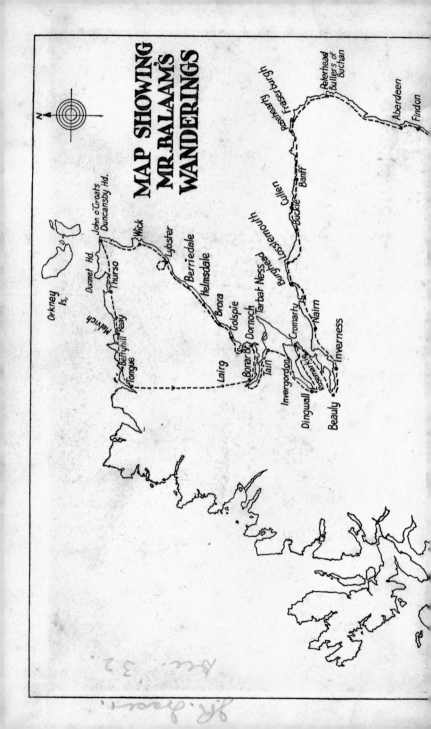

MAP SHOWING MR. BALAAM'S WANDERINGS

N

Orkney Is.

John o'Groats
Duncansby Hd.
Dunnet Hd.
Wick
Lybster
Thurso
Reay
Ben-y-hill
Melvich
Tongue
Lairg
Berriedale
Helmsdale
Brora
Golspie
Dornoch
Bonar Bdg.
Tain
Tarbat Ness
Cromarty
Invergordon
Dingwall
Rosemarkie
Nairn
Inverness
Beauly
Burghead
Lossiemouth
Buckie
Cullen
Banff
Fraserburgh
Rosehearty
Peterhead
Bullers of Buchan
Aberdeen
Findon